# FRESH, FUN PATTERNS TO QUILT IN A SNAP

# MINI QUILTS

## JODIE DAVIS & JAYNE DAVIS

The Taunton Press

The Taunton Press, Inc., 63 South Main Street, PO Box 5506,
Newtown, CT 06470-5506
e-mail: tp@taunton.com

Executive Editor: Shawna Mullen
Editor: Ashley Little
Copy editor: Candace B. Levy
Indexer: Jay Kreider
Art director: Rosalind Loeb Wanke
Photo editor: Erin Giunta
Layout coordinator: Amy Griffin
Illustrators: Jeffrey Rey
Front cover photos: (left column, top to bottom) © Scott Phillips;
(right colum, top to bottom) © Alexandra Grablewski
Back cover photos: (top row, left to right) © Scott Phillips;
(second row) © Alexandra Grablewski; (third row) © Jodie Davis;
(bottom row, left to right) © Scott Phillips
Interior photographers: © Alexandra Grablewski except for pp. 12–18, 26, 27, 30–33,
36, 37, 42, 46–53, 56, 57, 60, 61, 64–67, 70, 71, 74, 75, 78–81, 84–89, 91, 94–99, 102–105,
108–111, 114–117, 120–123, 126–129, 132–135, 141–143, 145, 147–149, 151, 152, 154,
155 © Jodie and Jayne Davis; pp. 24, 28, 34, 38, 44, 54, 58, 62, 68, 72, 76, 82, 92, 100, 106,
112, 118, 124, 130 © Scott Phillips

The following names/manufacturers appearing in Mini Quilts are trademarks:
AccuQuilt® GO!®, Aurifil™, Crayola®, Fons & Porter's®, FriXion®, GO! Baby®, Heirloom®,
Lite Steam-A-Seam2®, Steam-A-Seam2®, Warm & Natural®, The Warm Company™

Library of Congress Cataloging-in-Publication Data

Davis, Jodie, 1959-
  Mini quilts : fun patterns to quilt in a snap / Jodie Davis and Jayne Davis.
    pages cm
  ISBN 978-1-62113-796-2 (paperback)
  1. Miniature quilts. 2. Quilting--Patterns. I. Davis, Jayne S. II. Title.
  TT835.D37468 2014
  746.46--dc23
                    2013048550

Printed in the United States of America
10 9 8 7 6 5 4 3 2 1

# DEDICATION

To the Quilt Alliance for providing an enormous source of inspiration by preserving the stories of quilts and quiltmakers.

---

# ACKNOWLEDGMENTS

Thanks to every quilter—past, contemporary, and yet to be born—for contributing to the universal body of work, the unique sharing of ourselves that is quilting.

It's an honor to work with Taunton. For years I have admired the top-notch quality and leading edge design of everything they do. I was a charter subscriber to *Threads*, and when I bought and renovated my house, I devoured every issue of their home magazines.

Special thanks to the Taunton Press books staff, specifically: Shawna Mullen for her enthusiasm when first we met. Renee Neiger and Ashley Little for red inking with loving hands. Rosalind Wanke and Laura Palese for creating a wonderful interior and cover design. Erin Giunta for prettying up our photos. Amy Griffin and Laura Palese for skillfully laying out the book.

Thanks to my feline keyboard visitors Penny and Priscilla and Prudence for their typos (or the excuse of blaming them for them). And thanks to Candace Levy for correcting them.

# CONTENTS

# INTRODUCTION

How many times have you said to yourself, "So many quilts, so little time?" It's a blast to try new patterns, cut into another fat quarter of fabric from your favorite company, or delve into a new technique. But invariably that time factor creeps in. Have no fear, mini quilts are here!

## What Is a Mini Quilt?

Mini quilts may be small, but they have big personalities. They are a snap to make, and many take only a few evenings to finish. The mini quilts in this book are 16 in. square, and if bound, they measure 16½ in. square. (The only exceptions are Frayed Star (p. 44) and Swedish Folk Art in Felt (p. 72), which are 16 in. square after binding.)

I discovered the magic of a mini quilt when I became involved with the Quilt Alliance, a nonprofit that's devoted to archiving the stories of quilts and their makers. Each year the alliance holds a mini quilt contest as a fund-raiser. A few years ago, Luke Haynes, one of the board members, said he sees the contest as an opportunity to try a new technique. And I feel that mini quilts are also a great way to teach new techniques. After all, it's what I do as a quilting instructor and as one of the faces of QNNtv.com, an online quilting television website. It's why I like to call myself a "quilt enabler."

My stepmom, Jayne, is also an avid quilter, so I didn't have to twist her arm to help me design and make projects for this book. We had a great time sharing our favorite quilting tools and techniques with each other, and we are thrilled to have the opportunity to bring it all to you.

## Making the Most Out of Minis

Each mini quilt is a great punctuation point on its own, but as I discovered when I began making and collecting them, one quilt can soon turn into a large collection. Making them is rather addictive. Rather than hide all these minis in storage, I've provided a few projects that allow you to show off your bounty, fitting the quilts into your lifestyle. You'll find instructions for turning minis into pillows, totes, table runners, and more. Of course, if you fall head over heels for a particular technique, feel free to let those minis multiply and stitch them into a standard quilt.

Most of the quilts are designed for those with basic sewing skills. A few, such as the Seminole Patchwork (p. 38), require precision sewing skills, which means going slowly. Look for the skill level assigned to each project and choose those that are comfortable for you. As you gain skills, work your way up to more advanced projects.

To make the mini quilts, you will need common sewing gadgets, including a well-tuned sewing machine and cutting tools. If you're not familiar with the basics, review Part 1 (p. 4) to find out what types of tools you'll need to complete the minis. When something special is required to complete a quilt, I note that in the instructions.

Good things do come in small packages, even in quilting! I hope that you have as much fun creating a flock of minis as Jayne and I have had.

— *Jodie Davis*

# 1

## THE
## BASICS

# What You Need to Know

For most of the mini quilt patterns in this book, you'll need only basic sewing and quilting skills. In this chapter, I provide information on some of the techniques we use most frequently. Some of these may be new to you, while the descriptions of others may serve as more of a refresher course. One of the things I love about quilting is that there are always new things to learn. It's fun to hone our skills.

# Prepare to Quilt

You've decided to make a mini quilt. What's the next step? You'll need thread, basic quilting tools, and other equipment on hand so that making the quilt goes smoothly without last-minute trips to the store for this or that.

## BASIC QUILTING TOOLS

All the quilts and projects I share with you require basic quilting tools. If you have sewing experience, you may already own most of them. If you don't, make a list of the tools you need and pay a visit to your local craft store to get them. As you continue quilting you'll add more gadgets, but the following will get you started.

### ROTARY CUTTER

The rotary cutter revolutionized quilting. It made labor-intensive, hand cutting with scissors a task of the past. Be sure your cutter has a safety lock as it is extremely sharp. Also, always keep an extra blade on hand.

> **Tip** When you replace your rotary cutter blade, put the dull one in a another rotary cutter and use it to cut only paper. Never cut paper with your sharp blade as it will dull it very quickly.

### SELF-HEALING CUTTING MAT

Mats come in a variety of sizes. Buy the largest one that is usable in your work space and can easily be stored in your storage area. They come as large as 24 in. by 36 in., and most feature a 1-in. grid.

### SEE-THROUGH ACRYLIC RULER

See-through grid rulers come in several sizes. I use the 6 in. or 8 in. by 24 in. Other sizes can be useful, but either of these will suffice in all cases.

### SCISSORS

You'll find plenty of uses for a well-sharpened pair of scissors, from cutting out templates to trimming corners. They are always good to have around.

### PINS

Pins temporarily join fabrics and hold the pieces in place until you can permanently seam them together. Just remember: Never machine-stitch over pins because it can damage your needle, your machine, and even your fabric. Remove pins as you sew a seam. Glass-headed pins are a good choice because plastic heads can melt from an iron's heat when you're pressing.

### HAND-SEWING NEEDLES

Sharps needles—a type of hand-sewing needle—are a good multipurpose choice. There are specific needles for hand quilting and appliqué; they are noted in the instructions when needed.

> **Tip** Want to save yourself a lot of aggravation and squinty eyes when hand sewing? A fabulous tool is the Ultimate Needle Threader by Clover. Just pop in your needle, place your thread in the slot, and press the lever; you'll have a threaded needle almost instantly.

## IRON

An iron that can be used both dry and with steam works best for making quilts. Iron your fabric before quilting to remove wrinkles and prepare for accurate cutting. Wrinkled fabrics can result in pieces that do not measure correctly, throwing off the measurements of the entire quilt. You will also use an iron to press sewn seams, which gives your finished project a polished, professional look. An important quilting rule is *to press as you go*. The result is worth the extra effort.

Tip  Proper pressing is not the same as ironing. When ironing, you move the iron back and forth continuously on the fabric. When pressing, you set the iron down, then lift up and move to the next spot.

## PRESSING SURFACE

A sturdy movable ironing board is a must have. It's handy to be able to set up a pressing station next to your sewing machine so you can press as you go.

## MARKING TOOLS

There is no perfect fabric-marking technique that works in every circumstance. I've used dressmaker's carbon, purple disappearing pens, and chalk; finding just the right marking tool is an ongoing quest.

To make placement lines for the Hawaiian Gone Modern Stenciled Quilt (p. 54), I simply folded the square in half and in half again and pressed. For the In the Jungle Crayon Painting project (p. 58), Jayne used light pencil marks. The project

## To Wash or Not to Wash?

Whether to wash your fabric is an age-old question. Some quilters habitually wash every piece of fabric that walks in the door. Others wash selectively. So is it always necessary to wash your quilting fabrics?

It depends on how you are going to use the finished quilt. For a bed quilt or baby quilt that will be laundered over the years, wash and iron the fabric before beginning the project to avoid that dreaded puckered look after the first washing. On the other hand, if you want the look of a not-new quilt, leave your fabrics unwashed until the project is done. It's always a good idea to wash a swatch of any reds or dark colors in some hot water to see if the dye bleeds. If your project is a wall quilt that will never be laundered, why bother prewashing? Choose your comfort level and wash accordingly!

instructions will generally tell you the best technique to use.

My go-to marking tool of choice these days is the Pilot FriXion® erasable pen. This pen works like a regular pen, but the ink totally disappears when exposed to the heat of an iron. Experiment with different marking tools to find which one works best for you.

## KNOW YOUR SEWING MACHINE'S LITTLE HELPERS

Did you know your sewing machine may have some features that will help you sew more efficiently? Be sure to check out the manual to discover how to use the settings that quilters use all the time.

## NEEDLE DOWN

Most machines sold today have a button or screen icon that sets the needle to be either up or down in the fabric when you stop stitching. Setting the machine to needle down is incredibly helpful when turning corners, for appliqué, and in many other instances. Alternatively, if you turn the needle down setting to off, when you stop stitching, the needle will be up, allowing you to pull your fabric right out of the machine.

## PIVOT

Pivot is similar to the needle down, but with one big difference. When you finish stitching, the needle will remain down, plus the presser foot will rise. (You may even be able to control exactly how much it rises, depending on your machine.) This is pure pleasure when sewing curved seams and corners because it helps avoid continually moving the presser foot up and putting it down again.

## FASTENING STITCH

You may be familiar with the backstitch or back tacking. Today's machines offer an alternative function, the fastening stitch, that makes a few short stitches, thereby locking the threads. The benefit is that it's not as obvious as a backstitch.

## AUTOMATIC THREADER

The automatic threader? Best invention ever. Period! Ever tried to thread your sewing machine and failed again and again? This built-in gadget is a real time and irritation saver.

### Sewing Machine Maintenance

It's important to clean and maintain your sewing machine between projects to keep it working at its best. Follow the directions in the machine's manual to clean lint from the bobbin chase and feed dogs. Don't forget to remove threads and remnants that collect under the stitch plate and hook. Oil your machine, again following the manufacturer's instructions, and insert a new needle.

## WALKING FOOT

A walking foot "walks" over the fabric and prevents the upper fabric from sliding over the lower one by feeding fabric through the machine easily. It is also helpful when matching plaids and working with slippery fabrics like silk.

## TRACING PATTERNS

Sometimes quilters need to trace a pattern onto fabric (the In the Jungle Crayon Painting project, on p. 58, is one example). Here are two simple methods that I like to use.

## THE WINDOW METHOD

If you're working on a bright sunny day, tape your pattern to a window pane using masking or painters' tape—something that can be easily removed. Tape the fabric over the template and trace. It's so easy and no special equipment is required.

## THE LIGHT TABLE METHOD

If you have a light table, tracing patterns is a snap. Place the template and then fabric on the table, turn on the light, and trace. If you don't have a light table, you can improvise by using a glass-topped table. Place a small lamp under the table, tape the pattern and fabric on the glass, and trace. I have a clear extension table for my sewing machine and a mini fluorescent light that I use for tracing patterns.

## CUTTING FABRICS

Careful cutting is important for accurate results. You'll use a cutting mat, see-through ruler, and rotary cutter. Both the mat and the ruler have measurements printed on them. Once your fabric is squared up, decide which set of measurements you will use when cutting. Don't use the mat for one cut and the ruler for another. If there is even the tiniest variance between the two, it can cause real problems with stitching accuracy.

# Making the Quilt

There are many techniques used in quilting. In this section, I summarize a few of those I used most often in the patterns in this book. Some are done by machine and others are done by hand. Sometimes, we quilters do need to step away from the machine! In those instances, I let you know in the pattern if something must be hand-sewn.

## SQUARE KNOT

In quilting, a square knot is used to tie off two threads. Tie an overhand knot, passing the right-hand thread over and then under the thread in the left hand. Next, tie another overhand knot, passing the thread in your left hand over the thread in your right hand. Pull taut.

After tying the square knot a few times, it should come naturally to you. Simply remember: Right over left; left over right.

## THE SCANT ¼-IN. SEAM ALLOWANCE

A seam allowance is the width of fabric between the stitched line and the raw edge. Traditionally, a seam allowance in quilting is ¼ in. since a wider seam allowance in piecing would just create unnecessary bulk.

Your machine has a ¼-in. presser foot and a line on the throat plate, so why worry about the ¼ in.? Because, as famous quilting instructor Mary Ellen Hopkins used to say, we all have our own personal ¼-in. seam allowance.

The ¼-in. is different, depending on the way we sew and the tools we use. This fact may be the reason our quilt blocks turn out a little short or a bit too large. Even a slightly off ¼ in. seam allowance can become substantial when magnified over all of the blocks in a quilt.

What we try to achieve in our piecing is a scant ¼-in. seam. The *scant* part of the equation is what makes up for the turn in the fabric when you press your seam allowances to one side or press them open. If we sew a perfect ¼ in., it becomes more than ¼ in. when we press.

## SEWING A ¼-IN. SEAM

**PIECING PRESSER FOOT METHOD**

If you're using a presser foot made for piecing, you can adjust how you are aligning your fabric as you sew. As you stitch, align the fabric just a hair to the left of the right edge of the ¼-in. foot. This will give the pieces you are joining that scant breathing room.

## The ¼-In. Seam Test

Here's a test to try that just may surprise you. In fact, do it during your next sew-in with your friends. You'll be amazed at how many different ¼-in. seam allowances there will be!

Cut three pieces of fabric, each 2 in. by 3 in. Sew them together along their long edges using a ¼-in. seam allowance. Press the seam allowances to one side. Measure the width of the center strip. It should measure 1½ in. If your seam allowance was a perfect (or, actually, scant) ¼ in., you're a pro! If not, you discovered why your blocks are turning out small.

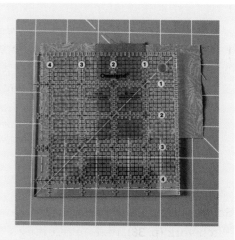

**STACKED TAPE GUIDE METHOD**

If you prefer not to rely on eyeballing your scant ¼-in. seam, try this method.

1. Lay a rotary cutting ruler under the presser foot so the needle will go down at the ¼-in. mark. Check the position by lowering the needle by hand just shy of the ruler (see the photo below).

2. Stick a 1-in. piece of masking tape to the bed of the machine, aligning it along the right-hand edge of the ruler. Sew another test, adjusting the tape as necessary. Once you have the placement correct, build up the stack of tape to form a ridge to butt your patchwork pieces against as you sew.

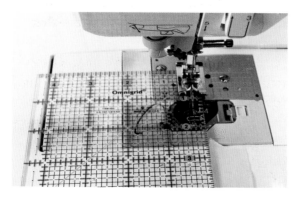

### MAKING YO-YOS

To make the Arts and Crafts Flowers project (p. 76) and Yo-Yo Quilt (p. 124), you will need to hand-sew yo-yos. Here's how:

1. Copy and cut out the yo-yo template for the project you are working on. A used file folder is the perfect weight for this.

2. Trace around the template onto your fabric and cut out the circle.

3. Cut a piece of thread 30 in. or more. Thread a needle, pulling the thread through and knotting the two ends together to double it.

4. Hold the circle so the wrong side faces you. Starting anywhere on the circle, turn the edge ¼ in. toward the center.

5. From the side facing you, insert the needle through both layers and come up through both layers. Continue with a running stitch of a scant ¼ in. long all the way around, finishing where you started.

6. Pull up on the stitches. Arrange the folds evenly, shaping the yo-yo. Pull the thread taut. Make a knot close to your stitching to secure.

### CHAINSTITCHING

Some mini quilts, like the Seminole Patchwork (p. 38), require seaming a large number of fabric pieces together. Instead of piecing them one at time, clipping the thread in between, try chainstitching. Chain-piecing segments of fabric together in assembly-line fashion saves you time and even thread.

Place the first pair of pieces together with right sides facing and the raw edges even. Stitch an accurate ¼ in. seam. At the end of the seam, stop sewing. Without lifting the presser foot, feed the next pair into the machine right after the first set. Continue in this manner, feeding pairs into the machine to form a chain. When they are all sewn, clip the threads between the pieces.

# Finish the Quilt

## QUILT BACKINGS

Once the quilt top is all finished, you need to think about the back of the quilt. Generally we choose coordinating fabrics for the backing and binding of our quilts. This is especially important if the quilt will be used as a throw or bed quilt because the backing will be visible. If the backing will never be seen, any fabric will do, including plain muslin. Backings can be complex or simple in design. Like many aspects of quilt design, it's up to you.

**FELT BACKINGS**

Quilts are usually intended for beds, but we often hang mini quilts like pictures. If you'd like your mini quilt to be stiffer so it hangs squarely on the wall, use either wool or felt as a backing. Or, if you have completed the quilt already and are finding it a little floppy, simply fuse a piece of felt to the back using a fusible webbing. Voilà! Your quilt will stand soldier straight.

**FALSE BACKINGS**

Many quilters put as much effort into their backings as they do the fronts of their quilts. In fact, it was the back of a quilt made by my mom's best friend—a maze with a mouse in the center and a kitty in one corner—that propelled me into quilting.

For some of the projects, I instruct you to layer your quilt top, batting, and backing to make a quilt sandwich and sew right through. But doing this can sometimes leave an ugly back, like the Thread Painting mini (p. 28). If that gives you the willies, simply

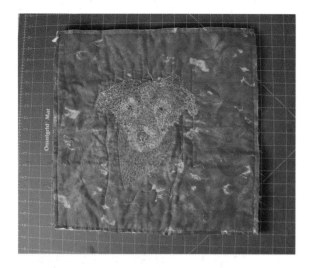

add another backing to the quilt before you sew on the binding. Use spray baste or safety pins to hold it in place and baste around the edges of the quilt less than ¼ in. in from the raw edges. Then bind as usual.

## HOW TO MAKE A QUILT SANDWICH

By definition, a quilt is two pieces of fabric—the quilt top and the backing—with something soft in between. To get that soft layer, quilters use batting.

A quilt sandwich consists of the three layers that are quilted together: a quilt top, batting, and backing. Packaged battings are readily available at your local quilt shop, fabric store, and online. You'll find a wide range of fiber content, such as cotton, polyester, wool, and silk and combinations of all these. For my mini quilts, I used either Heirloom® cotton batting by Hobbs Bonded Fibers or Warm & Natural® by the Warm Company™.

To build your quilt sandwich, start from the bottom layer and work up. There are three ways to hold the layers together: basting spray, safety pins, and hand basting. Is one method better than another? Not really. Try them all and see what works best for you.

### USING BASTING SPRAY

1. Place the batting on a covered work space. (Newspapers, newsprint, or an old sheet all work as coverings.) Spray one side of the batting lightly with basting spray.

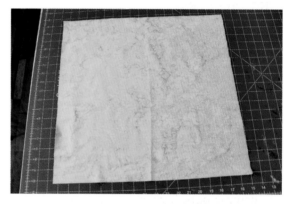

2. Place the backing on top with the wrong side facing the batting. Smooth it out with your hands and then turn the pieces over so the batting side faces up.

3. Spray the batting lightly with basting spray. Spread the quilt top carefully over the batting. Smooth it out.

### USING SAFETY PINS

1. Assemble your quilt sandwich.

2. Pin through all the layers, placing pins about 6 in. apart.

### HAND BASTING

1. Assemble your quilt sandwich.

2. Baste the layers together using long running stitches (about ½ in. long), sewing both horizontal and vertical rows 4 in. to 5 in. apart. No need to be neat because you are holding the layers together only temporarily. The basting threads will be removed after quilting.

## SQUARING UP YOUR MINI QUILT

Before binding your quilt, you need to make sure it's the right size. Squaring up is a very important last step in constructing quilt blocks. Let's say you are making a quilt of 10-in. blocks that is six blocks wide and six blocks tall. If some or all of your block measurements are off even a little, your entire quilt will be off.

That said, if all the blocks are consistently ¼ in. too large, your quilt will simply be larger than anticipated. As long as you're consistent, you should be okay.

All the mini quilts in this book are designed to be 16 in. square, with an extra ½ in. square for binding. When you finish your project, measure its height and width. If it's a little wonky—say 16⅓ in. by 16¾ in.—then make the mini 16½ in. square. But if the quilt is 16¼ in. square, it's already square and won't be joined to another piece, so don't fret.

If your mini quilt is not 16 in. square before binding, see if you can figure out why. Is it your piecing? Did your quilting draw up the fabric? It's all about learning from your mistakes!

Always square up your quilted mini before binding. Here's how: lay the mini on your cutting mat. You'll quickly see any offending edges. Use your rotary cutter, cutting mat, and see-through ruler to carefully trim the quilt into a perfect square.

## BINDING SMALL QUILTS

Throughout this book, a regular double-fold straight-of-grain binding is used. This is the binding most often used by quilters. It gives a strong, neat finish and wears well, which is very important for a quilt that is used frequently, such as a bed quilt. In addition, we have mixed things up with a self-binding for the Frayed Star mini (p. 44) and a hand-stitched blanket-stitch binding for the Swedish Folk Art in Felt quilt (p. 72). Instructions for the traditional double-fold binding are here. You will find instructions for the other bindings with the quilt project.

For the mini quilts you will need only two strips of fabric: 2¼ in. long by the width of your fabric (typically, 42 in. to 45 in.). Packaged double-fold binding is available to buy, but the fabric will often be a different quality from your quilt fabric, resulting in a less-than-professional-looking finished project. Plus, it's so simple to make your own binding!

## DOUBLE-FOLD BINDING

1. Cut the ends of the strips at a 45-degree angle. Match the short end of one strip to the short end of the other strip. Seam.

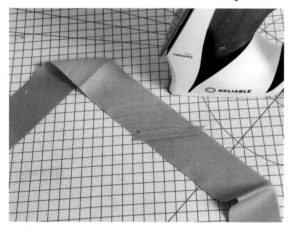

2. Press the seam open. Press the strip in half lengthwise.

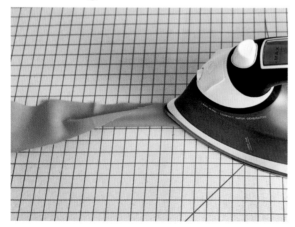

3. Begin stitching the binding to the quilt edge halfway between two corners. Leave a 6-in.-long tail at the top before starting to stitch. Stop and backstitch ¼ in. from the bottom corner.

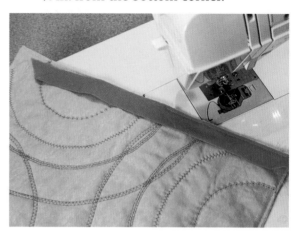

4. Turn the quilt. Fold up the binding strip vertically.

**5.** Fold the binding down. Starting at the top raw edge of the quilt, stitch, backstitch, and continue stitching down to the next corner. Stop ¼ in. from the edge and backstitch again.

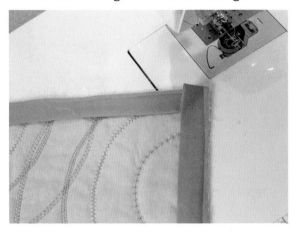

**6.** Repeat for the remaining corners. When you return to the side you started on, stitch the binding to the first few inches of that edge.

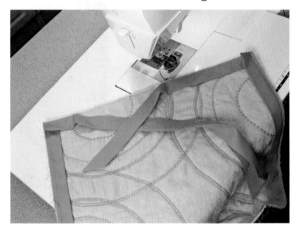

**7.** Overlap the ends of the binding. Trim so they overlap 2¼ in.

**8.** Open the left strip and turn.

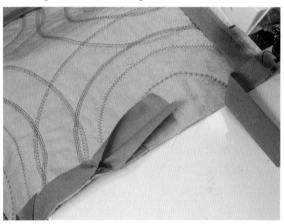

**9.** Open the right strip.

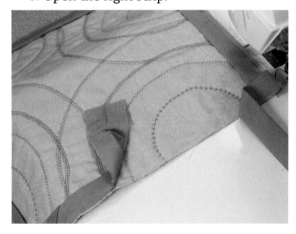

10. Mark a 45-degree line on the right strip. Match the strips perpendicularly, right sides together. Pin. Stitch on the line.

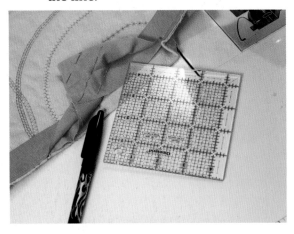

11. Trim the binding edges. Press the seam allowance open.

12. Refold the binding. Press. Finish the stitching on the edge of the quilt.

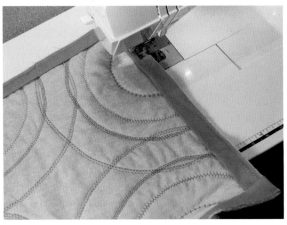

13. Turn the binding to the back of the quilt and pin in place. Hand-stitch the binding using a blind stitch. This stitch gives a neat, finished look in the back.

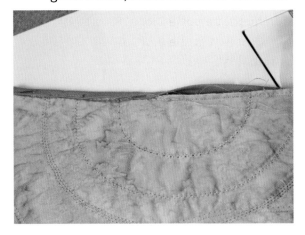

## Display Your Minis

If you've made several mini quilts, you may be wondering what to do with them. If you don't want to turn your minis into a larger quilt, there are a couple of creative ways you can display them.

- Display minis in multiples by hanging them on the wall in groups of two, three, or four. Minis can also be connected in chain fashion using supplies like ribbons or rings.

- Hang minis on a clothesline using clothespins or just attach clothespins directly to a wall.

- Frame your mini as you would a piece of art. Frame it yourself or take it to a framer for a professional look. The added benefit is that the quilt will be protected from dust.

- Dress up a tabletop. If you have a side table that is just about the same size as your quilt (about 16 in.), order a piece of glass cut to fit the top. Place the mini under the glass to create an unexpected display.

- Skip the batting, backing, and binding and instead stretch the mini quilt top over an artist's canvas. Staple the quilt to the back, pulling it taut. Hang the quilt as is or have it framed.

### Quilted Background

The folks at Moda Fabrics kindly created the most fabulous method for hanging the contest quilts for the Quilt Alliance. Not only did the display look great but it was easy to take down and put back up as the mini quilts traveled from quilt show to quilt show. They simply used quilted panels! For the exhibits, the panels hung on the drape apparatus commonly found at convention centers. For home display, you could quilt plain fabric, add a sleeve, and hang it from a rod. Then pin or baste your mini quilts to the larger quilt.

# 2

## MINI QUILT PATTERNS & TECHNIQUES

# Making Mini Quilts

Because you've opened this book, you undoubtedly share the love of sewing that Jayne and I enjoy. Part of the fun is in having the things we make around us. "Yes, I made that," is a great thing to be able to say. Not only are these mini quilts custom made but they also go with our homes in a very personal way. For instance, I turned the Hawaiian Gone Modern Stenciled Quilt (p. 54) into pillows for my bed that coordinate with the lamps in the room.

And then there is gifting of items that are handmade with thought and love for the recipient. The grandma to Woody, a border collie, parades every visitor into her guest room to see the Thread Painting mini (p. 28) I gave her for Christmas. She wouldn't do that if it were a photograph.

Both of these facets of quilts are what make quilting so special. Add the element of connecting people through memories, and quilts become downright powerful. A great example is The Today's Crazy Quilt (p. 106) where Jayne used a photo of her great-aunt. What better way to remember her aunt than through a photo quilt on her wall?

What you can do with each of these minis is endless. Enjoy making, displaying, and giving mini quilts!

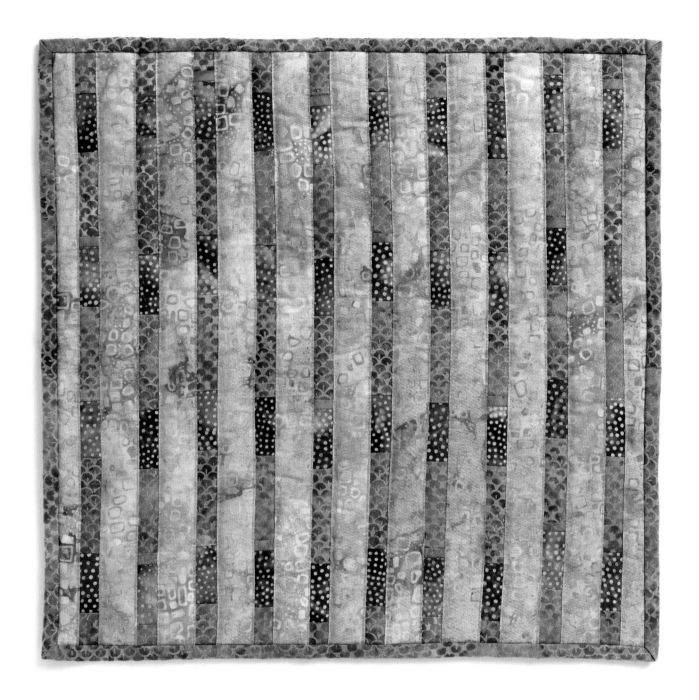

**THE DESIGN:** Inspiration is all around us. All we have to do is open our eyes. I like linear shapes. No matter how ancient the object, it has a modern look to me. See the way the bricks are laid in a wall? That's a linear design. A rusty heating grate was the inspiration for this quilt. I saw sunshine and shadows and that brief period when they blend together day after day.

# Picky Piecing
## MODERN GRAPHIC QUILT

DESIGNER: Jayne Davis

I guess you could call me a picky piecer. I like seams to join exactly and lines to be straight. Remember the old saying, Anything worth doing is worth doing well? I'm a firm believer. Fabric is not cheap, and your time has value. If you're going to spend all that money and time making a quilt, you should be picky about your piecing. With this mini quilt, you'll become an expert at precision piecing. Here is an opportunity to hone your skills and find that it doesn't take all that much extra effort to do the job right.

SKILL LEVEL: Intermediate | THE TECHNIQUE: Chainstitching (p. 13)

## What You'll Need

- ¾ yd. light colored batik fabric (A) for the wide strips and backing
- Fat quarter blue batik fabric (B) for the pieced strips and binding
- Fat eighth brown batik fabric (C) for the pieced strips
- Scrap orange fabric (D) for highlights in the pieced strips
- 21-in. by 20-in. batting

## What You'll Learn

You will be working with small pieces of fabric to create a striking graphic design. On p. 140 is a lovely tote bag made using two mini quilt tops in this design, along with full directions. Chainstitching is the fastest way to piece the strips.

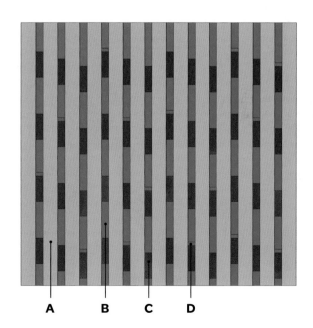

A    B    C    D

# Fabric Cutting Chart

Cut your fabric according to this chart.

| | Fabric | Measurements | No. of Pieces |
|---|---|---|---|
| FOR THE BACKING | A | 21" by 20" | 1 |
| THE WIDE STRIPS | A | 1½" by 18" | 13 |
| FOR THE BINDING | B | 2¼" by 20" | 4 |
| FOR THE PIECED STRIPS | B | 1" by 3" | 60 |
| | C | 1" by 2¼" | 48 |
| | D | 1" square | 15 |

## PIECE THE STRIPS

1. Start piecing with fabric D. Take a 1-in. piece of blue fabric B and lay it right side up. Fold an orange fabric D piece in half lengthwise with wrong sides facing and line it up with the short, top edge of fabric B, raw edges together. Top with a brown fabric C piece right side down, making sure the top raw edges are all even. Machine stitch. Repeat until all the orange fabric D pieces are used. Cut these 15 chained pieces apart and set aside.

   Next, chainstitch the 1-in. blue fabric B pieces and the remaining brown fabric C pieces in pairs. You'll have 12 blue fabric B pieces left. Cut the chained pieces apart.

## SEW THE STRIPS TOGETHER

2. Sew these elements together to make the pieced strips. Follow the drawing on p. 25 to distribute the highlight pieces. End each strip with one of the remaining 1-in. blue fabric B pieces. Press the seams toward the dark fabric, making sure the folded edge of each fabric D piece turns up and covers the fabric B piece.

3. Stitch all the pieces together following drawing on p. 25.

   Begin joining the light fabric A strips and the pieced strips. Separate the pieced strips into 3 groups. Cut ½ in. off the top edge of the strips in group 1. Cut ¼ in. off the top edge of group 2. Do nothing to group 3. Join the strips as shown in the drawing, alternating among the groups of pieced strips so the colors ripple. After each seam is sewn, stop and press the seam toward the light strip.

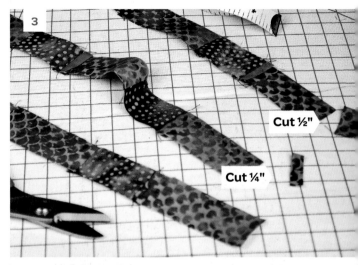

Cut ½"

Cut ¼"

## QUILT AND BIND

4. Once all the strips are sewn together, follow the instructions on p. 14 to make a quilt sandwich. To quilt, begin in the center and work outward. Stitch in the light fabric A strip very close to each side of the pieced strip, but do not stitch directly in the seamline.

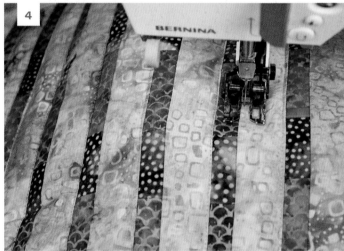

5. Using your rotary cutter, trim the quilt to 16 in. square.

6. If you are binding the quilt, make a continuous binding from the 2¼-in. strips of blue fabric B. Then bind the quilt as instructed on p. 15.

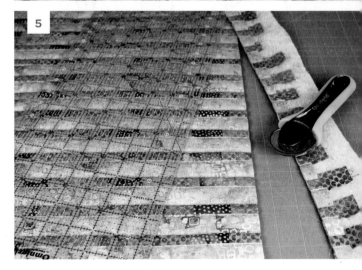

**THE DESIGN:** Artsy as it looks, thread painting is not rocket science. It's a simple matter of color blocking the image into shapes. My subject was a dear 14-year-old dog named Woody. His winter fuzziness called to my thread rack, and the simplicity of his coloring made a great introduction to thread painting. I used only five threads: black, white, red, gray, and a variegated white with gray for the patches around his eyes. For the background, I chose various tone-on-tone fabrics in white to serve as a gentle frame for Woody.

# THREAD PAINTING

DESIGNER: Jodie Davis

Thread isn't just for sewing seams together! With an endless palette of threads, we sewers have a medium in our sewing room that opens amazing opportunities. It's the neatest (in both senses of the word) "paint" and has the added benefit of providing dimension to our work. Plus thread can be layered to create shading, which adds great realism to our quilts. As you select fabrics for the appliqué shapes, remember that you will be nearly covering them with stitches. I agonized over Woody's eye patches, going to several shops to try to find just the right fabric. When I finished the piece, I realized it didn't matter. The pattern of the fabric was muted by my stitching. All that angst for no reason!

---

**SKILL LEVEL:** Intermediate │ **THE TECHNIQUES:** Free-motion thread painting (p. 31), creating an appliqué pattern (p. 30), fusible appliqué (p. 31)

---

## What You'll Need

- Thread Painting Template (p. 161) or a photograph of your pet against a contrasting background
- White tone-on-tone scrap fabrics for the background (pieces A, B, C, D, and E)
- Black, red, white, red, gray, and variegated white fabric scraps or scraps that match your pet for the appliqué fabrics
- ½ yd. fabric for the border pieces
- Fat quarter fabric for the backing
- ¼ yd. fabric for the binding
- 16½-in.-square batting
- Fusible web such as Steam-A-Seam2®
- 40-weight thread in black, white, red, gray, and a variegated white or thread that matches your pet

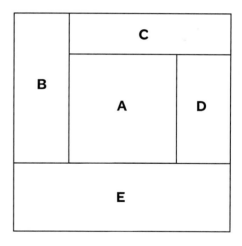

## What You'll Learn

You'll turn a photo into an appliqué pattern and fuse the color-blocked fabric patches to a background. Free-motion quilting and a palette of threads will turn your simple design into art!

# Fabric Cutting Chart

Cut your fabric according to this chart.

| Fabric | Measurements |
|---|---|
| Piece A | 8½" square |
| Piece B | 4½" by 11½" |
| Piece C | 3½" by 12½" |
| Piece D | 4½" by 8½" |
| Piece E | 5½" by 16½" |
| Border | 4" by 26" (cut 4) |
| Backing | 16½" square |
| Binding | 2¼" by 42" to 45" (cut 2) |

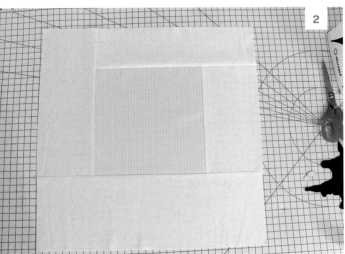

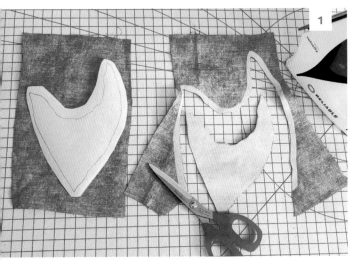

## MAKE THE APPLIQUÉ PIECES

1. Copy the Thread Painting template, on p. 161, and enlarge it by 300 percent. Cut out each appliqué piece.

   Or make your own pattern: Use your home printer to enlarge a photograph of your pet so that it fits within the 8-in. square piece A, which will be the center of the quilt. Lay the fusible web on top of your pattern and trace one of the shapes. Trim about ¼ in. or more outside of your traced line. Repeat for all of the shapes. Remove the unmarked waxed paper–like piece and lightly press the fusible web to the back of your appliqué fabrics. Cut along the marked lines, creating your appliqué pieces.

## MAKE THE QUILT TOP

2. Using the border fabric and the layout on p. 29 as guides, stitch piece D to the center square of background piece A. Press the seam to one side. Stitch piece C to pieces D and A. Add piece B, and finally piece E. Press as you go. When the quilt top is completed, place it right side up on your pressing surface.

Tip  To avoid gaps between your appliqué pieces, try making the pieces slightly larger where they overlap. For example, I made Woody's white head a little larger on the edges where his ears are and then put the ears on top. Don't worry too much about this, though, because you'll be covering everything with thread anyway!

## FUSE THE APPLIQUÉ IN PLACE

3. Lay out the appliqué shapes on the quilt fabric, following photo 3 for placement. Follow the manufacturer's instructions for fusing the silhouette shape to the background.

## MAKE THE THREAD PAINTING

4. Follow the instructions on p. 14 to make a quilt sandwich. Wind bobbins with each of the threads you'll be using to stitch. Choose a free-motion presser foot for your sewing machine. (I like the open-toe type so I can see my stitching as I go.) Drop your feed dogs.

5. Choose which area you will start thread painting and thread your sewing machine accordingly. Let your needle down and then up, so that you can pull the thread tails to the top. Now you're ready to stitch.

For my thread painting I used only straight stitches. My machine has a speed dial, which I used to keep from going too fast and getting ahead of myself. Start stitching up and down, working side to side on the appliqué shape. Don't worry about having perfectly straight stitches. Work horizontally, filling the shape in rows, overlapping the previous row. Then go up a row, turning the work as you stitch. Never put the needle down; this is free-motion sewing.

**6** After filling in the shape, you may wish to add texture, like I did with Woody's fuzziness round his ears. Use straight stitches, stitching in the direction of the hair.

**7** Stitch the white part of the fur in the center of Woody's face, making short vertical lines of stitching to reflect the shorter fur around his nose.

**8** For the eye, stitch slowly with black thread, one stitch at a time, around the eye. Go around several times.

Tip Depending on your pet's fur, you may wish to go back with another thread color to better create the texture and color of your dog or cat.

9. Add the pupil, stitching up and down until it is as large as in the photo.

10. For the nose, I sewed a curlicue to add nostrils, creating a more realistic look.

11. To give a hint of the body, trace the body outline from your appliqué pieces onto the quilt and stitch up and down along the traced lines. Trim all thread tails.

## TRIM AND BIND

12. Trim the quilt to 16½ in. square. If you are binding the quilt, make a continuous binding from the 2¼-in. strips of fabric. Then bind the quilt as instructed on p. 15.

---

**NOTE:** Since you're stitching through all layers, you'll end up with an ugly back. I figured no one would take the quilt off the wall to discover this, so I didn't worry about it. If you prefer a pretty back for your quilt, check out how to create a false backing on p. 13.

---

**THE DESIGN:** Interlocking circles are a familiar theme in quilting. The Double Wedding Ring pattern is the first example that comes to mind; it's an all-time favorite of many quilters, myself included. When designing this project, I played on a similar image of interwoven circles. At first I drafted a symmetrical design, but then I mixed it up by setting it a bit out of alignment.

# Decorative
# STITCHED CIRCLES

DESIGNER: Jodie Davis

How many great decorative stitches does your sewing machine have? Have you ever used those stitches? Let this project be your excuse! You can customize the design by choosing your stitches, thread colors, textures, and of course, your fabric. I found this cotton damask-type fabric in my stash. Because it goes well with the couch in my den, I created the mini quilt with the intension of turning it into a pillow later. (For instructions for making the pillow, see Mini Quilt Pillow, on p. 144.)

SKILL LEVEL: Easy | THE TECHNIQUE: Decorative stitches (p. 37)

## What You'll Need

- **Decorative Stitched Circles template (p. 156)**
- **Fat quarter of fabric for the quilt top**
- **Fat quarter fabric for the backing**
- **¼ yd. fabric for the binding**
- **17½-in.-square batting**
- **Four colors of thread for decorative stitching**

---

**NOTE:** Because you'll need to run the stitches past the 16-in. square, I have allowed extra fabric to stop and start on. You'll get a nice decorative stitch going before stitching on the quilt top, which will be invisible when finished.

---

## What You'll Learn

If you are a pretty good sewing machine driver, this project will be easy. This mini involves drawing circles on your quilt top and then steering around them.

### Choosing Thread

For this project, I used a 40-weight cotton Mako from Aurifil™ in the bobbin and as my top thread. Check your machine to see if you need to change your upper thread tension. Test rayon, metallic, and even wool thread to see what works. You can also pick a heavier thread weight; in fact, I have doubled 50-weight thread, running it from two spools and into a size 90 needle, when I've needed a heftier effect. Make a little test quilt sandwich and try out your stitches and thread before sewing on your quilt.

# Fabric Cutting Chart

Cut your fabric according to this chart.

| Fabric | Measurements |
|--------|-------------|
| Quilt Top | 17½" square |
| Backing | 17½" square |
| Binding | 2¼" long by 42" to 45" (cut 2) |

## TRACE THE CIRCLES

1. Copy the Decorative Stitched Circles template on p. 156, and enlarge it by 400 percent one quarter of the pattern at a time. Tape the pattern together. Transfer the circle designs to the fabric using the tracing method of your choice (see p. 9 for techniques). Mark the outer edge of the finished 16-in. square too, so you'll know where to start and stop your stitching.

## QUILT

2. Follow the instructions on p. 14 to make a quilt sandwich.

---

**NOTE:** If you'd like, use scraps of fabric to make a practice mini quilt sandwich so you can test your stitches before committing to your real quilt. Experiment with the different stitches on your machine. You may wish to loosen your top tension, which hides your bobbin thread and gives a smoother-looking stitch, but most likely that won't be necessary.

---

Tip  Layering the quilt sandwich before stitching the circles eliminates the need for a stabilizer. If you were to sew the circles on just the quilt top, you would need something to stabilize the fabric. The method used here allows the decorative stitching to show on the back. Mine looks great, so it's not a problem. If you choose a different fabric from that on the front, you could have a reversible quilt!

3. Wind bobbins with each of the threads you'll be using to stitch the circles. Choose a presser foot that will allow you to see your traced line well. An open-toe appliqué foot works well, though your regular sewing foot may be your favorite.

Choose the thread color and style of stitch you wish to use for the outer, largest circles.

Start your stitching about ½ in. outside the markings designating the 16-in. square. Stitch along the traced line, gently following the curve.

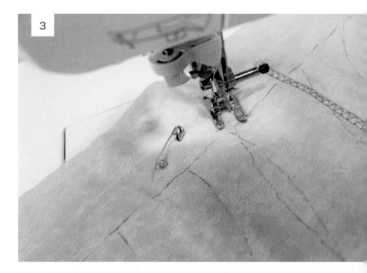

4. As you complete stitching the arc, continue about ½ in. past the traced line that indicates the edge of the 16-in. square, sewing into the seam allowance. Sew each of the largest arcs.

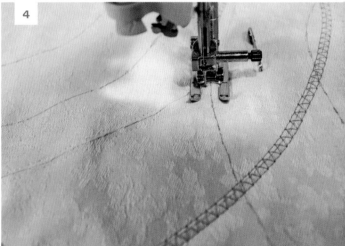

5. Switch thread and change your sewing machine to the decorative stitch you've chosen for the next smaller circles and stitch. Repeat for the last two sets of arcs. Baste along the outer edge of the quilt, ⅛ in. outside of the marked edge, which designates the 16-in. edge. Trim to 16½ in. square.

## BIND

6. If you are binding the quilt, make a continuous binding from the 2¼-in. strips of fabric. Then bind the quilt as instructed on p. 15.

**THE DESIGN:** For this project I chose batik fabrics to produce colorful results. Two different patterns are used in this quilt. Three Seminole bands are featured separated with plain bands of color. Pattern 1 comes first, then pattern 2, followed by pattern 1 again. Each pattern band is made up of three fabrics: a light-, a medium-, and a dark-colored fabric.

This project requires a lot of sewing, so I recommend you do a quick maintenance on your sewing machine before starting. See p. 10 for maintenance tips.

# SEMINOLE PATCHWORK

DESIGNER: Jayne Davis

Seminole Patchwork differs from the more familiar types of patchwork because strips of fabric are cut across the width of the fabric, sewn together, cut into segments, and then rearranged and sewn back together into wonderful patterns. The number of combinations is limitless. The results look very complicated but are in fact quite simple to do.

Seminole Patchwork has always been a machine technique. The Seminole and Miccosukee Indians lived in the Florida swamps. In the 1880s, they obtained hand-cranked sewing machines and fabric from traders. Authentic Seminole patterns were worked in solid colors and often used bands of baby rickrack stitched on the plain bands. Today we use lots of different fabrics, all with interesting results.

---

**SKILL LEVEL:** Intermediate | **THE TECHNIQUES:** Chainstitching (p. 13), piecing (p. 11)

---

## What You'll Need

- ¾ yd. yellow fabric for the strips and backing
- ¼ yd. orange fabric for the strips (do not use a fat quarter)
- ⅓ yd. blue fabric for the strips and binding
- 18-in.-square batting
- Thread to match the yellow fabric

## What You'll Learn

Seminole Patchwork looks complicated, but it is quite easy to do. The secret is to make sure all seams are accurately sewn at ¼ in. Pressing is also paramount to getting good results. Set up a pressing station next to your sewing machine and press the seams as you sew.

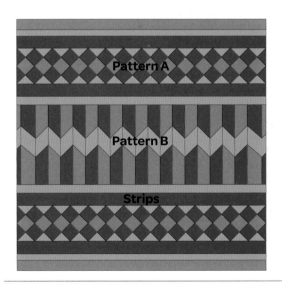

**NOTE:** Quilting can reduce the finished quilt's size, so it's better to have a few extra inches of batting that you can trim away.

# Fabric Cutting Chart

Cut your fabric according to this chart, cutting across the width of the fabric.

| FABRIC | Pattern A | | | Pattern B | | | Strips | | | Binding | Backing |
|---|---|---|---|---|---|---|---|---|---|---|---|
| | Yellow | Orange | Blue | Yellow | Orange | Blue | Yellow | Orange | Blue | Blue | Yellow |
| NUMBER OF PIECES | 4 | 2 | 4 | 1 | 1 | 1 | 4 | 2 | 4 | 2 | 1 |
| MEASUREMENTS | 1½" by 42" to 45" | 1¼" by 42" to 45" | 1¼" by 42" to 45" | 1¼" by 42" to 45" | 1¼" by 42" to 45" | 2" by 42" to 45" | 1" by 17" | 1½" by 17" | 1½" by 17" | 2¼" by 42" | 18" square to 45" |

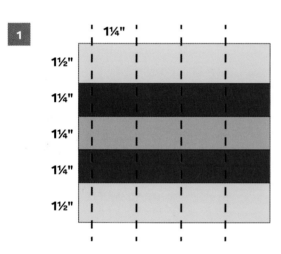

## PIECING PATTERN A

1. Sew two yellow, two blue, and one orange strip together in the order shown in drawing 1. Press the seams open. Repeat for the second band. Next, cut each band into 1¼-in. segments until you have used all the pattern A band fabric. Be very careful that each segment is exactly 1¼ in.

---

**NOTE:** You will need to make two pattern A bands: one for the top of the mini quilt and the other for the bottom.

---

2. Sew together 16 segments on top and 16 segments on the bottom, as shown in drawing 2. Be sure the seams match exactly and stitch. After sewing the segments together, press the seam allowances all in one direction.

3. Line up your cutting ruler along the top edge of the band, adding a ¼-in. seam allowance above the top row of squares. Trim the pattern A band as shown in drawing 3. Repeat for the bottom edge.

### PIECING PATTERN B

4. Sew the three strips for pattern B together in the order shown in drawing 4. Press the seams open. Fold the completed strip in half and press.

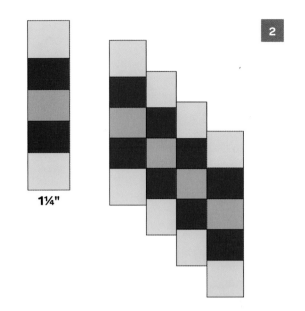

1¼"

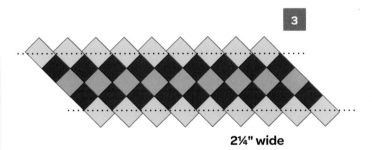

2¼" wide

## Matching Seamlines

It takes a little time, but I have a method that guarantees the seamlines match. Place right sides together. Place a straight pin through both seamlines at the seam allowance. Pin the pieces together, removing the original pins. Stitch, removing pins as you go. When you open up the piece, you will have perfectly matched seams.

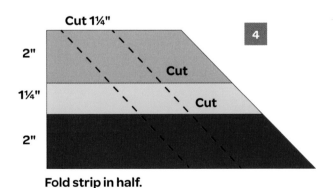

Cut 1¼"

2"

Cut

1¼"

Cut

2"

Fold strip in half.

5. Your cutting mat has 45-degree lines marked on it. Place the folded strip on a straight line and your ruler on a diagonal line. Cut the strip into 1¼-in. segments as shown in photo 5. Be very careful you are accurate.

6. Lay out all the segments as shown in photo 6 to confirm that the zigzag line is correct. This will save you a lot of grief if you should get one segment in the wrong order.

Tip  Move your cut edge to the diagonal line on your mat each time you cut to make sure the cuts are accurate. It's so easy to make a cutting mistake. If you continue across inaccurately, the mistake will be compounded, and the segments will never go together correctly.

7. Sew the segments together and press all the seams in one direction. Trim the completed strip, cutting the points off the top and bottom edges.

### PIECE THE QUILT

8. Using the quilt top photo on p. 38 as your guide, sew the bands and Seminole strips together in order, as shown. Press all the seams to one side away from the patchwork bands and then press the completed quilt top.

### QUILT AND BIND

9. Follow the instructions on p. 14 to make a quilt sandwich. Attach a walking foot to your machine. Using matching thread, quilt in the ditch (see p. 169) on each side of the yellow fabric bands. This gives you eight quilting lines.

   If you are binding the quilt, make a continuous binding from the two binding strips. Then bind the quilt as instructed on p. 15.

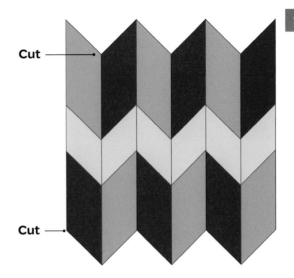

Cut

Cut

7

**THE DESIGN:** Here's how inspiration turns into design. I saw a picture of a strip-pieced quilt with star shapes made from soft, muted colors. The fabric was actually fabric selvedges. I remembered that image when someone started posting photos of vintage chenille comforters on Pinterest. Years ago I saw how quilters once made chenille. It all came together in my head and a light bulb went off. I had a new technique to try!

# FRAYED STAR

DESIGNER: Jodie Davis

Does the word *chenille* conjure up thoughts of cozy bedrooms with tufted bed spreads? You can achieve a similar effect by layering fabrics, stitching through them, and then clipping through the layers. The magic happens when the piece is washed and dried. To achieve a nice, soft chenille, use top-quality cotton fabric. A loosely woven cotton won't stay as tight, resulting in a less-pleasing look to your finished project. I used brown-, yellow-, orange-, green-, and rust-colored fabrics for the layers of my star. If you're feeling adventurous, experiment with different color schemes for your mini quilt.

SKILL LEVEL: Easy   |   THE TECHNIQUE: Making chenille fabric (p. 46)

## What You'll Need

- **Frayed Star template (p. 158)**
- **¾ yd. brown fabric**
- **¾ yd. yellow fabric**
- **¾ yd. orange fabric**
- **¾ yd. green fabric**
- **¾ yd. rust fabric**
- **Fat quarter of fabric for the backing**
- **16½-in.-square batting**

**NOTE:** Because the backing is folded over to create the binding, the finished measurement of this mini quilt is 16 in. square.

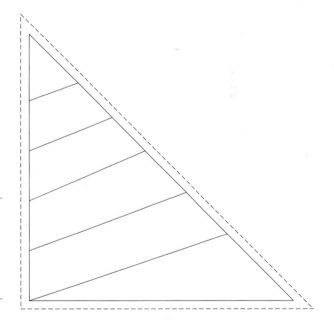

## What You'll Learn

This mini will teach you how to stack and sew multiple layers of fabric that form a design when cut. The trick is deciding where each layer of fabric shows up to form a colorful pattern.

# Fabric Cutting Chart

Cut your fabric according to this chart.

| Fabric | Measurements | No. of Pieces |
|--------|-------------|---------------|
| Brown | 10" by 12" | 8 |
| Yellow | 10" by 12" | 8 |
| Orange | 10" by 12" | 8 |
| Green | 10" by 12" | 8 |
| Rust | 10" by 12" | 8 |
| Backing | 16½" square | 1 |

## PREPARE THE PATTERN

1. Copy the Frayed Star templates on p. 158, and enlarge them by 400 percent.

   For each of the eight rectangles that you have chosen for your top fabric (I used brown for mine), mark horizontal lines across them as follows: 2½ in. from the top, a line 1½ in. below that, and three more lines 1½ in. below. Note that the top fabric will be the center of the star.

   You may wish to mark the top with a T to avoid confusion later. This will be at the outside edge of the finished quilt.

## PREPARE THE CHENILLE LAYERS

2. Layer the colored fabrics into eight stacks, all in the same color order. Place the marked fabric on top, for the top layer and center of the star. Use safety pins to hold the layers together.

---

**NOTE:** My colors, top to bottom, are brown, yellow, orange, green, and rust.

---

## STITCH THE CHENILLE LAYERS

3. Set your machine to a 3.5 stitch length. Stitch along the marked lines from raw edge of the fabric to raw edge.

Tip For my quilt, I used a 40-weight cotton thread for both topstitching the four layers together and the quilting. The heavier weight provides a heftier, more substantial look.

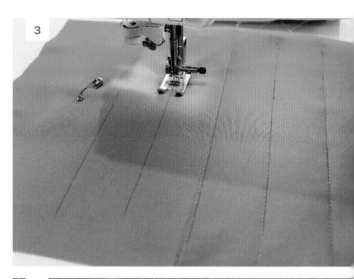

## TRIM THE CHENILLE LAYERS

4. Place the template over one stitched stack, lining up the lines on the pattern with those you have stitched on the fabric. Don't worry if they no longer match up perfectly. The lines on the quilt may have been distorted by your sewing through the layers. Using a ruler and rotary cutter, trim along the pattern edges.

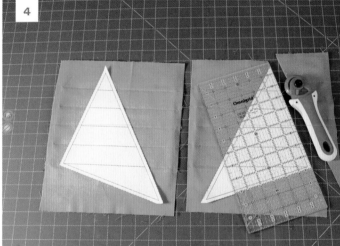

## CLIP THE CHENILLE LAYERS

5. Start your chenille clipping between the bottom two lines of stitching. Trim through only the top layer of fabric, about ¼ in. from the stitching on each side.

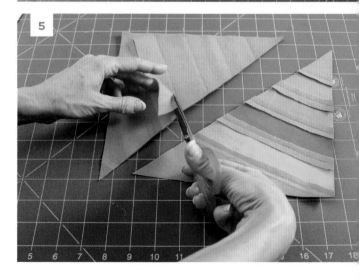

6. Clipping reveals the second, yellow, layer underneath.

7. Working toward the top, trim between the stitching through two layers: the top brown and the yellow just below it. The orange layer will be revealed.

8. Next, trim between the stitching through three layers: the top brown, the yellow just below it, and the orange. Now it's the green fabric's turn to be revealed.

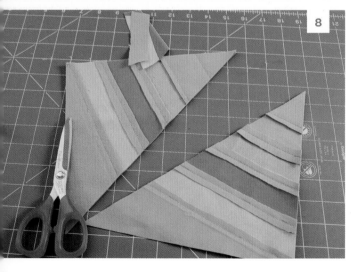

9. Finally, cut through four layers: the top brown and the yellow, orange, and green below. The rust fabric will now make its appearance.

10. At the bottom end the piece, trim all the layers except the brown fabric to ¼ in. from the stitching. This will reduce the bulk at the center of the star, making the piecing easier and neater.

11. Repeat steps 4 to 10 for each of the remaining stitched fabric stacks.

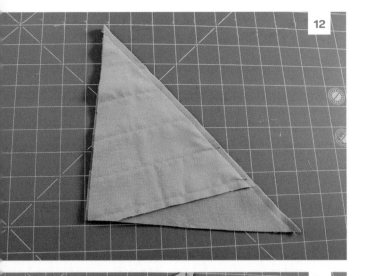

## CONSTRUCT THE STAR

12. Match two of the eight sections carefully.

13. Stitch the edges together. Press the seam open.

14. Trim the dog ears (see the Glossary on p. 168). Repeat steps 12 and 13 to make four sets.

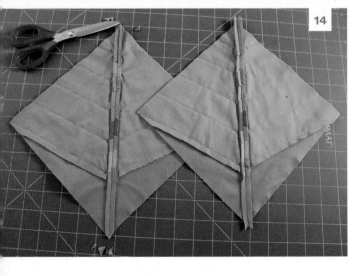

15. Match the edges of two sets. Stitch. Press the seam allowances open. Repeat for the remaining two sets.

16. Match and stitch the two halves of the Frayed Star quilt together. Stitch. Press the seam open.

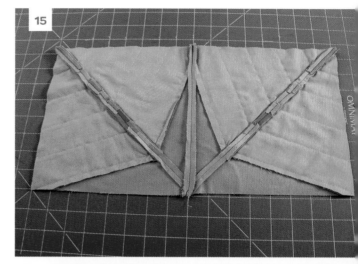

## MARK THE QUILT FOR QUILTING

**17.** Using your rotary cutting ruler, draw a line ½ in. in from the inner most topstitching of one section of the star. Make another line ½ in. in from this one. Repeat for a total of three lines. Do the same for the remaining seven sections of the star.

## MAKE THE QUILT SANDWICH

**18.** Place the backing fabric wrong side up on a table. Trim a ¾-in. square out of one corner. (The backing will be turned to the front later to form the binding.) Repeat to trim the remaining three corners.

**19.** Follow the instructions on p. 14 to make a quilt sandwich.

## QUILT AND BIND

**20.** Quilt each of the three inner stars using a 3.5 stitch length and following the lines you drew in step 17.

**21.** Turn one edge of the backing to the front of the quilt, overlapping about ½ in. Topstitch ¼ in. from the edge, backstitching at the beginning and ends of your stitching. Repeat for the remaining three edges.

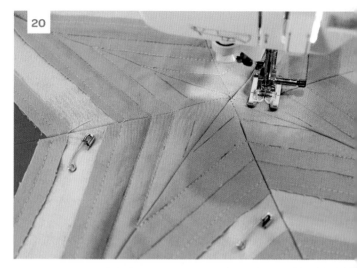

**THE DESIGN:** Inspired by Hawaiian quilts, this mini quilt quickly turned into a more modern interpretation. Hawaiian quilts are gorgeous examples of handwork mastery. Extremely simple in design, a shape is usually made out of a solid-color fabric and appliquéd to a plain background, which is most often white or cream. The result is simple and graphic.

# Hawaiian Gone Modern
# STENCILED QUILT

DESIGNER: Jodie Davis

For this project I applied paint to fabric using stencils for a nice clean effect. Stencils are quick and easy to cut and so much faster than appliqué. As long as you don't glob your paint on, the fabric will not be stiff. It will take you no time to become proficient at fabric painting. In fact, this may be the easiest project in the book. Stenciling results in a mark-of-the-hand look that appliqué doesn't offer. With so many mass-produced products out there, something made by human hands is appreciated that much more. I turned this pattern into a pillow and also used it to create a lovely table runner. (For the Stenciled Table Runner, see p. 153; for the Mini Quilt Pillow, see p. 144.)

SKILL LEVEL: Easy  |  THE TECHNIQUES: Stenciling on fabric (p. 56), hand embroidery running stitch (p. 57)

## What You'll Need

- Hawaiian Gone Modern Stenciled Quilt templates (p. 158)
- Fat quarter high-quality gold quilters' cotton for the quilt top Fat quarter gold fabric for the backing
- ¼ yd. gold fabric for the binding
- 16½-in.-square batting
- White embroidery floss to outline the stencils
- Spray fixative (optional)
- Stencil plastic or file folders for the templates
- 5 bottles acrylic paint in various colors
- Stencil brush, natural sponge, or other special paint applicator

## What You'll Learn

Create your own fabric design by making a stencil and applying acrylic paint to fabric using a sponge. Then, after creating the quilt sandwich, add detail using embroidery floss and a simple running stitch.

# Fabric Cutting Chart

Cut your fabric according to this chart.

| Fabric | Measurements | No. of Pieces |
|---|---|---|
| Quilt top | 16½ in. square | 1 |
| Backing | 16½ in. square | 1 |
| Binding | 2¾ in. by 45 in. | 2 |

## STENCIL

1.  Copy the two Hawaiian Gone Modern Stenciled Quilt templates on p. 158 and enlarge the red flower by 400 percent and the yellow flower by 200 percent. Trace the pattern onto the stencil plastic, using your favorite technique (see p. 10 for tracing methods). Cut the stencil shapes as designated on the pattern, creating a separate stencil for each color. Leave the other areas marked for placement.

    To create placement lines for your stenciling, fold the quilt top fabric in half and in half again. Press. On each line, make a dot 2¾ in. down from the raw edge. This marks the placement for the center of the yellow flower.

2.  Starting with whichever stencil you wish, line up the edge of the stencil to the folded lines so that it will appear in one-quarter of the quilt top. Dab the sponge or brush into the paint, then onto a paper towel. You want it to be fairly dry so the paint doesn't run under the stencil. Dab gently into the area to be painted, building the color gradually.

3. Repeat step 2 for the remaining quarters of the quilt. Then repeat for the remaining stencils. For the yellow flower, line it up as indicated on the stencil template with the center on your dot. Stencil the entire flower and then the red circle on top.

> **Tip** Test on scrap fabric first. You will get the feel for how much paint to load onto your stenciling tool. If you find your stencil slipping as you dab, you can use a temporary spray fixative on the underside of the stencil to hold it in place.

## QUILT AND BIND

4. Lay the backing fabric wrong side up on a table. Follow the instructions on p. 14 to make a quilt sandwich.

5. Work a running stitch with the embroidery floss around the design elements, starting and ending with a square knot (see p. 11) on the back of the work or buried in the backing.

6. Continue to work a running stitch around all four squares.

7. If you are binding the quilt, make a continuous binding from the 2¼-in. strips of fabric. Then bind the quilt as instructed on p. 15.

**THE DESIGN:** This is coloring after all, so I wanted the project to have a coloring-book look. This technique was popular back in the 1920s and 1930s and generally featured children and pets, with the occasional pretty lady. I wanted a more whimsical look and *The Jungle Book* came to mind. Do giraffes really live in the jungle? I don't think so. But who cares? Let's call this artistic license.

# In the Jungle
# CRAYON PAINTING

DESIGNER: Jayne Davis

Remember how you once loved to color and prided yourself on staying inside the lines? Add a grown-up twist to a childhood pastime. Using this technique, you can permanently paint using crayons on fabric rather than on paper. To add extra punch, outline the figures with a simple embroidery running stitch. Add colorful borders and you have a quilt top that's ready to quilt and bind in no time.

**SKILL LEVEL:** Easy | **THE TECHNIQUES:** Crayon painting (p. 60), transferring patterns onto fabric (p. 9)

## What You'll Need

- **In the Jungle templates (p. 157)**
- **13-in. piece unbleached muslin for the jungle scene**
- **½ yd. green batik fabric for the backing and borders**
- **¼ yd. black print for the binding and inner border (do not use a fat quarter)**
- **18-in.-square piece batting**
- **1 skein black 6-strand embroidery floss**
- **62-count box of Crayola® crayons**
- **Plain paper, such as newsprint, for setting the colors**

## What You'll Learn

This project could not be easier. You'll learn how to transfer patterns onto your fabric, plus how to get the best effect from your crayons (do you really need a lesson in coloring?). You'll also punch up the look using a black running stitch.

# Fabric Cutting Chart

Cut your fabric according to this chart.

| Fabric | Measurements | No. of Pieces |
|---|---|---|
| Black print binding | 2¼" by 42" to 45" | 2 |
| Black print inner border | 1" by 16" | 4 |
| Green backing | 18" square | 1 |
| Green borders | 2¼" by 16" | 2 |
| Green borders | 2¼" by 13" | 2 |

## PREPARE FOR CRAYON PAINTING

1. Enlarging by 200 percent, copy the In the Jungle templates on p. 157 for the jungle scene. Join the four pieces where marked, attaching A to B, and so on, following the instructions on the templates. To trace the pattern onto the muslin, center the pattern under the muslin, tape it in place, and trace it using your favorite marking pen or pencil. (See p. 9 for information on tracing methods.)

## COLOR AND SET THE DESIGN

2. Color the designs, staying within the lines. Use a circular motion so you'll have good coverage without obvious stripes.

3. Place the fabric between two pieces of plain paper with the design face up. Press with a hot iron to heat-set the color. Next, using two strands of the six-strand embroidery floss, embroider around the designs with a simple running stitch. Put several stitches on the needle at one time, then pull the thread through.

Tip When you're embroidering and moving from one motif to another, thread your way through existing stitches on the back side.

## ADD THE BORDER

4. Trim the muslin to exactly 13 in. square. Press the inner border strips in half lengthwise. Place an inner border strip along each edge of the muslin, raw edges together. Hand-baste in place so it will not slip when the outer border is added.

5. Stitch the 13-in.-long green strips to opposite sides, making sure the folded side of the inner borders face the jungle scene. Then stitch the longer strips to opposite sides. Press well.

## QUILT AND BIND

6. Follow the instructions on p. 14 to make a quilt sandwich. Machine-quilt two rows of stitching in the outer border. Trim to 16 in. square.

7. If you are binding the quilt, make a continuous binding from the 2¼-in. strips of fabric. Then bind the quilt as instructed on p. 15.

**THE DESIGN:** Originally, silhouette makers cut the profiles freehand while looking directly at their subject. I make it easier with the help of technology, by working from a photograph. Children and pets are the traditional subjects for silhouettes, but you can use a building, skyline, row of trees, or your house as a subject.

This design also uses a mitered border. Yes, you could stitch a border strip to each side of your quilt center, then a strip entirely across the top and bottom. But creating a mitered border gives your piece a great finished look—and you gain a new sewing skill!

# Traditional
# SILHOUETTE IN FABRIC

DESIGNER: Jodie Davis

When I was growing up, my parents displayed silhouettes of my sisters and me over their bed. A black frame touched with a hint of gold gilt surrounded our hand-cut paper profiles. Simple! My animals are my children, so I have been itching to create silhouettes of my horsies to hang over my bed. And because I'm a quilter, here they are in fabric!

**SKILL LEVEL:** Easy | **THE TECHNIQUES:** Raw edge stitching (p. 65), twin needle stitching (p. 67), simple inset border (p. 66), mitered border (p. 66)

## What You'll Need

- Profile photo of your child or pet that has good contrast between the subject and the background or Horse Silhouette template (p. 161)
- Fat quarter white background fabric for the silhouette
- Fat quarter black fabric for the silhouette
- ½ yd. brown fabric for the border
- ¼ yd. multicolored fabric for the inset
- Fat quarter fabric for the backing
- ¼ yd. black fabric for the binding
- 17½-in.-square batting
- Fusible web, such as Steam-A-Seam2
- Black thread for topstitching silhouette
- Size 4 wide twin needle

## What You'll Learn

Using the twin needle is as simple as threading two needles and stitching a straight line. The effect belies the ease of the technique. Mitered borders are a great skill to add to your sewing repertoire, giving your work that well-finished look.

# Fabric Cutting Chart

Cut your fabric according to this chart.

| Piece | Measurements | No. of Pieces |
|---|---|---|
| Silhouette | 10" square | 1 |
| Silhouette background | 10½" square | 1 |
| Backing | 17½" square | 1 |
| Border | 4" by 26" | 4 |
| Inset border | 1½" by 10 ½" | 4 |
| Binding | 2½" by 76" | 1 |

## PREPARE THE SILHOUETTE

1. Use a printer to enlarge your photo to fit within the 10-in. square that will be the center of the quilt. If you use the Horse Silhouette template on p. 161, which is of Tina, my miniature horse, enlarge it by 200 percent.

**NOTE:** On the finished quilt, the silhouette will be the mirror image of the original picture or template.

2. Lay the fusible web on top of your template and trace the shape (see p. 10 for tracing techniques). Trim ¼ in. or more outside of the traced line. Remove the unmarked waxed paper–like piece and lightly press the web to the back of your black fabric. Cut along the marked lines, creating the silhouette.

## FUSE THE SILHOUETTE

3. Follow manufacturer's instructions for fusing the silhouette shape to the background fabric. Using a 1.4 stitch length, straight stitch just inside the raw edge of the silhouette using the black thread. Stitch slowly! If you have a speed control bar on your machine, use it.

> **Tip**  The secret to stitching around the fused, cutout shape is to stitch slowly with a shortened stitch length—sometimes almost one stitch at a time. You will be stitching close to the edge of irregular shapes, so *slow* is the operative word.

## QUILT

4. Place the backing fabric wrong side up on your work surface. Place the batting on top, aligning the raw edges. Don't worry if the edges do not line up exactly because there is extra, which will be cut away later. Lay the silhouette on top, right side up, and centered. Pin in place.

5. Using a 3.0 machine stitch, quilt around the silhouette on the background fabric through all layers.

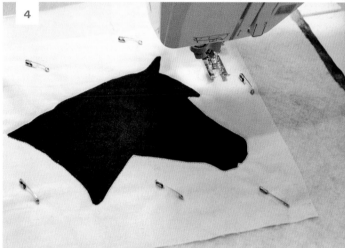

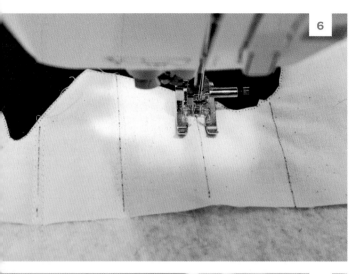

**6.** Using an iron-erasable pen draw a vertical line down the center of your quilt or where it doesn't cross your design in a strange place. For example, it wouldn't look good if the line bisected the top of a person's head. Draw lines to each side, 1½ in. away.

Insert the twin needle into your sewing machine and thread. Using a stitch length of 3.0, stitch along the drawn lines, keeping them in between the two needles. It's easiest to start in the middle and work to the edges.

**7.** Leave long thread tails. Pull the thread ends along the silhouette edge to the back of the quilt and tie them when you finish your stitching.

### STITCH THE INSET BORDER

**8.** Press the inset border strips in half lengthwise. Baste two strips to the sides of the muslin. Baste the remaining two inset border strips to the top and bottom of the muslin.

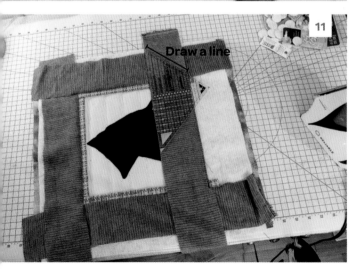

### STITCH THE MITERED BORDER

**9.** Attach the border strips, starting and ending ¼ in. in from the corner of the background fabric. You can use the stitching on the inset border strips as your stop and start points.

**10.** Stitch the border strips to the four edges of the muslin.

**11.** To make mitered corners, open one of the border strips so it is wrong side up and free of wrinkles. Lay a 45-degree ruler on top, placing the long edge along

Draw a line

the outer (unstitched) edge of the border strip. Match the end of the stitching to the stitching line on the ruler as shown in the photo 11 on the facing page, adding a ¼-in. seam. Draw a line.

12. Repeat for the adjoining strip. Cut along the drawn lines.

    Fold the quilt in half from that corner to the adjacent corner. Carefully match the angled ends of the border strips. Stitch from the point where they meet to the pointy ends of the strip. Press the raw edges to one side.

### BIND

13. Trim the quilt to 16½ in. If you are binding the quilt, make a continuous binding from the 2½-in. strips of fabric. Then bind the quilt as instructed on p. 15.

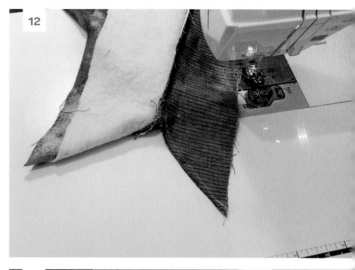

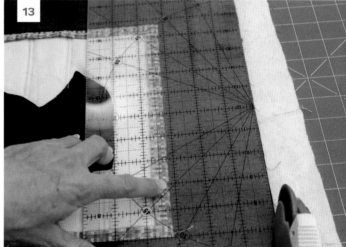

---

**NOTE:** Because you're stitching through all layers with the twin needle you'll end up with an ugly back. If you prefer a pretty back for your quilt, check out how to make a false backing on p. 13.

---

## Twin Needle Stitching

For the background in the square behind my horsies, I chose to quilt double rows of stitches. Called *twin needle stitching*, this is another one of those things our machines can do but that most of us have never tried. Once you do, you may find that it's useful in a lot of situations. For this technique, you will need two spool holders for you sewing machine. Your manual will tell you how to set up your sewing machine for twin needle stitching.

**THE DESIGN:** The fabric is the star here, so keep the design simple. I chose to make this mini quilt from sixteen 4½-in. squares, half a light color (in this instance white) and half a dark color (a deep rich red). To add a little extra interest, I added a contrasting circle at each intersection topped with a button. For the backing and binding, I chose a paisley cotton that picks up the wool colors. All the layers are tied together through the buttons.

# ALL TIED UP IN WOOL

DESIGNER: Jayne Davis

The feel of wool conjures up walks in the woods and cozy evenings by the fire. It warms our bodies, and it's a tactile fiber that feels just plain cuddly to the touch. So I decided to make a mini quilt out of wool and tie the quilt together rather than quilt it with stitches. Then I added a button or two for pizzazz.

**SKILL LEVEL:** Easy | **THE TECHNIQUES:** Working with wool (p. 70), how to tie a quilt (p. 71), embellishing a quilt with buttons (p. 71)

## What You'll Need

- All Tied Up in Wool template (p. 156)
- ¼ yd. dark-colored wool
- ¼ yd. light-colored wool
- 8-in.-square black wool
- ⅔ yd. cotton fabric for the backing and binding (this fabric should pick up the wool colors used)
- 18-in.-square batting
- 1 sheet fusible web such as Lite Steam-A-Seam2®
- 1 skein six-strand cotton embroidery floss to match the dark wool
- 1 skein black six-strand cotton embroidery floss
- 1 medium embroidery needle
- 1 large tapestry needle
- 9 ¾-in. or 1-in. buttons with two holes
- Pressing cloth, such as a white cotton dish cloth

## What You'll Learn

You'll become comfortable working with wool. You'll also hone your skills in stitching a simple hand-embroidered blanket stitch. With this mini quilt, you'll be tying through buttons for an added touch—and it's much faster than quilting!

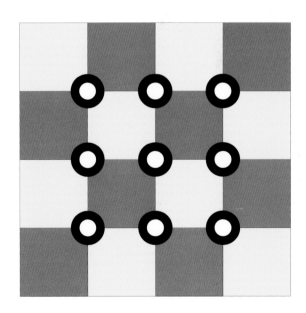

# Fabric Cutting Chart

Cut your fabric according to this chart.

|  | Fabric | Measurements | No. of Pieces |
|---|---|---|---|
| **FOR THE SQUARES** | Dark wool | 4½" square | 8 |
|  | Light wool | 4½" square | 8 |
| **FOR THE BACKING** | Backing fabric | 18" square | 1 |
| **FOR THE BINDING** | Binding Fabric | 2¼" by 42" to 45" | 2 |

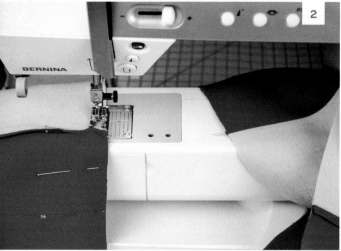

## PREPARE THE PATTERN

1. Using the 2-in. All Tied Up in Wool template on p. 156, trace nine circles onto the fusible web following the manufacturer's directions (for tracing methods, see p. 10).

   Again, following manufacturer's directions, remove the paper backing and finger-press the circles onto the wrong side of the black wool.

   Cut out the circles along the traced lines.

2. Chainstitch (see p. 13) the 4½-in. squares together following the sequence shown in the layout drawing on p. 69. Begin by stitching a dark and light square together. Then chainstitch two of these units together. You'll have four strips of four squares each.

   Press the seams open. When you turn the strips over and press the seams on the right side, use a pressing cloth.

   **Tip** It's important to use a pressing cloth with wool, because the high heat needed to make steam can scorch or leave a shine on the fabric.

Following the layout drawing, stitch the rows together. Carefully press the seams open.

3. Remove the backing from the fusible web and place each black circle on the checkerboard, as shown in the drawing on p. 69. Finger-press them in place and then fuse them in following the manufacturer's directions. Don't forget to use a pressing cloth.

Tip  Place the iron down and lift it up when fusing. Don't move it back and forth as you would when ironing.

4. Blanket stitch around each circle by hand (see p. 75 for instructions) or machine. Stitch as close to the edge as possible.

## ATTACH THE BUTTONS

5. Make a quilt sandwich (p. 14), centering your mini quilt on the batting. Thread the tapestry needle with all six strands of the dark embroidery floss and stitch a button in the middle of each circle.

   To finish, pull the floss taut and cut it off at about 3 in. long. Tie the ends in a firm square knot (see p. 11). Trim the thread ends to ½ in.

6. Carefully trim the tied quilt to 16-in. square. If you are binding the quilt, make a continuous binding from the 2¼-in. strips of fabric. Then bind the quilt as instructed on p. 15.

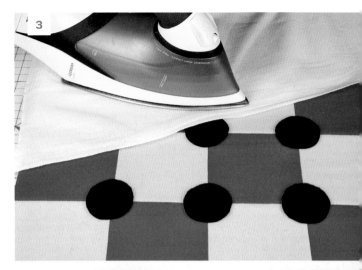

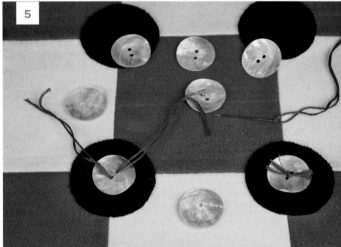

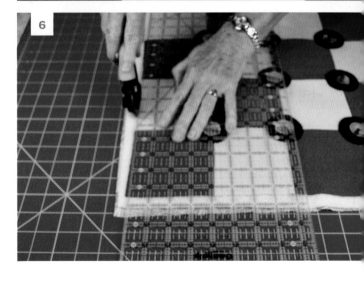

THE DESIGN: For inspiration, I paged through books and websites on folk art. And there it was—the symbol of Sweden—the Dala horse. It's a charming, carved wooden horse that is painted shiny red and trimmed with bright designs. I knew it would translate perfectly into an all-felt mini quilt with simple hand-appliquéd details and finished off with a felt backing. The mini is held together with a hand-stitched blanket stitch. And the trims? Buttons, of course! Here's a chance to use those bright baubles in your button box or head to your local fabric shop for a button-shopping spree.

# Swedish
# FOLK ART IN FELT

DESIGNER: Jayne Davis

Folk art has a charm all its own. It reminds me of earlier times, and the designs make me smile. I knew I wanted to work with felt—dense, thick wool felt, the kind you want to touch and bury your nose in.

This is a really simple project. Just cut out the pattern pieces, stitch down the pieces in their proper places on the background with a blanket stitch, and embellish. I plan to put this charmer on the wall in my sewing studio/office/guest room. Wherever it is, it will definitely keep a smile on my face.

---

SKILL LEVEL: Easy │ THE TECHNIQUES: Freezer paper pattern transfers (p. 74), embroidering a blanket stitch (p. 75), embellishing with buttons (p. 75), felting wool (below)

---

## What You'll Need

- Swedish Folk Art in Felt template (p. 160)
- ½ yd. off-white 100 percent wool felt
- Scraps of 100 percent wool felt in blue, yellow, green, and red
- 5 skeins six-strand embroidery floss, one in each color to match the felt
- Embroidery needle
- Three ¾-in. buttons for the saddle
- Five ⅝-in. buttons for the girth
- One 1½-in. black button for the eye
- Fourteen 1-in. buttons for the borders
- 12-in.-long piece freezer paper for templates

---

**NOTE:** Because the quilt edge is hand-embroidered with a blanket stitch instead of binding, the finished measurement of this mini quilt is 16 in. square.

---

## What You'll Learn

Freezer paper is your new best friend for making templates. It is easily ironed in place, so it doesn't move when tracing or cutting around it.

## Felting Wool

Yes, you can felt your own wool, but it works only with 100 percent wool. Here's how:

- Fill your washing machine with its hottest water; add a small amount of detergent and the fabric.
- Run the machine through a full cycle.
- Place the wool in the dryer at its highest setting.

If the wool hasn't felted to your satisfaction, repeat.

# Fabric Cutting Chart

Cut your fabric according to this chart.

| Fabric | Measurements |
|--------|-------------|
| Off-white felt | 16" square |
| Off-white felt | 17" square |
| Blue felt | 10" by 16" |
| Yellow felt | 4" by 15" |
| Green felt | 3" by 6" |
| Red felt | 14" by 9" |

## TRANSFER AND CUT THE PATTERN

1. Cut the freezer paper into two 8½-in. by 11-in. sheets. Press the sheets on the dull side with a dry iron so they will lay flat. Place the freezer paper sheets in your copier so that it will print on the dull side, and copy the Swedish Folk Art in Felt template from p. 160, enlarging by 200 percent.

2. Cut out the pattern pieces. For each piece, place the pattern shiny side down on the proper color felt and press with a dry iron. This will make the pattern stick to the felt. (Don't worry; it will easily peel off.)

   Cut out the felt pattern pieces using sharp scissors.

## EMBROIDER

3. Place the pattern pieces onto the backing felt, following the photo of the finished quilt on p. 72. Hand-baste close to the edge of each piece so it will stay in place as you work the blanket stitches. Begin embroidering around all the pieces using two strands of the six-strand embroidery floss. To start, put a knot in the thread and enter the fabric from the wrong side, leaving the knot hidden at the back.

Tip If you'd rather not hand embroider, machine-stitch the pieces in place using a straight stitch close to the edges. Practice on scraps until happy with the results. I experimented using my machine's built-in blanket stitch, but the layers of felt were too thick and the stitch wasn't wide enough.

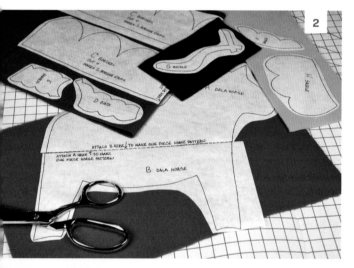

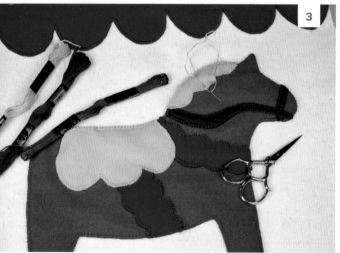

4. The blanket stitch is easy to do. Referring to drawing 4 come up at point 1. Holding the thread down with your thumb, go down at point 2 and come back up at point 3 with the needle tip over the thread. Pull the stitch into place.

5. Repeat, stitching so the bottom legs of the stitch form an outline along the raw edge of the appliqué shape. To end your stitching, simply slide the needle under an inch of worked stitches on the wrong side and cut the thread.

6. Lay out your button selection. Sew the buttons in place using matching thread. Go through the buttons' holes two times, knotting the thread on the back side.

### TRIM AND BIND

7. Follow the instruction on p. 14 to make a quilt sandwich, but use only the quilt top and backing. Using your rotary cutter, trim to 16 in. square.

---

**NOTE:** This mini quilt has no batting layer, so there's no need to quilt it.

---

Finish the edge with a hand-embroidered blanket stitch. There is no need to bind this quilt.

If you machine-stitched the appliqués, you'll want to finish the mini quilt with a double-fold fabric binding, as shown on p. 16, to keep the style consistent.

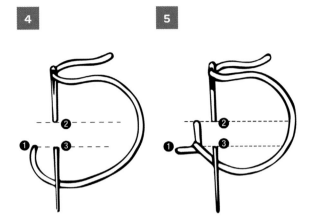

**THE DESIGN:** Jodie developed this curved paper piecing technique to add texture to what is normally a flat piece. I love the added dimension these inserts give to a design. I chose brilliant colors, but maybe you'd prefer a cooler range. The choice is up to you. Just be sure to pick a dark, a medium, and a light fabric plus a coordinating fabric for the top and bottom bands.

# Arts and Crafts
# FLOWERS

DESIGNER: Jayne Davis

The Arts and Crafts movement flourished between 1860 and 1910. Themes were taken from nature and the designs were reduced to their simplest forms. This flower design doesn't look like any flower you've ever seen in your garden. Notice the texture the curved paper piecing and fluffy yo-yos give the leaves and flowers. Each flower panel is pieced in parts and then quilted. Make your own version as a tribute to the Arts and Crafts movement.

SKILL LEVEL: Intermediate | THE TECHNIQUES: Curved paper piecing (p. 79), yo-yos (p. 12)

## What You'll Need

- **Arts and Crafts templates (pp. 162–163)**
- **½ yd. dark fabric for two flower panels and backing**
- **½ yd. medium fabric for one flower panel and binding**
- **Fat quarter green fabric for the leaves and stems**
- **Fat quarter light fabric for the flowers**
- **Fat quarter coordinating fabric for the top and bottom bands**
- **18-in.-square batting**
- **8½-in. by 11-in. newsprint or computer paper (though it's more difficult to tear away) for the templates**

## What You'll Learn

Paper piecing will be a piece of cake after you've completed this mini quilt. Plus you'll learn the curved paper piecing technique that adds dimension to your quilting projects. You'll also learn how to make yo-yos.

# Fabric Cutting Chart

Cut your fabric according to this chart.

| Piece | Measurements | No. of Pieces |
|---|---|---|
| Backing | 18" square | 1 |
| Binding | 2¼" by 42" to 45" | 2 |
| Horizontal bands | 3½" by 16½" | 2 |

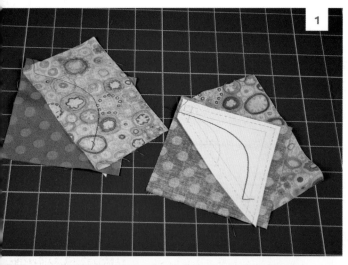

## PREPARE AND CUT THE PATTERN

1. Copy the Arts and Crafts Flowers tem-plates on pp. 162–163 enlarging 200 percent onto the newsprint, printing three copies of each page.

   After cutting the templates out, set your machine for a stitch length of 18 to 20 stitches per inch. The shorter stitch length is stronger and won't come apart when you tear away the paper backing.

   Start with patterns G, H, I, and J. For J, cut a piece of the medium background fabric about a ¼ in. larger than the pattern. Cut a piece of the flower fabric about the same size. Place the pattern printed side up on the wrong side of the background fabric and the flower fabric under the background fabric with right sides of the two fabrics together. Stitch along the curved line, making sure there is plenty of flower fabric to fold back after trimming. Photo 1 shows both sides of the unit after stitching.

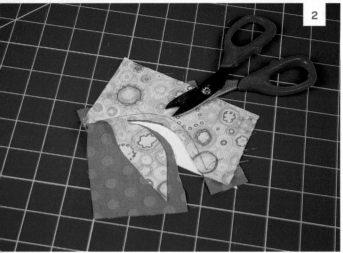

2. Trim the seam allowance of the curved stitching to ¼ in. Be sure not to cut the paper, just the fabrics.

## MAKE THE FLOWER PANELS

3. Fold the flower fabric over the seam. Fold the pleats toward the center, pinning each pleat in place to make the fabric lie flat. I used a total of six pleats, with three facing left and three facing right.

4. Using the longest stitch possible on your sewing machine, machine baste all around the pattern piece, securing the pleats and removing the pins as you go. (Never stitch over pins.) Repeat with pattern pieces B, C, D, and E, pleating the leaf sections using the leaf and background fabrics. After stitching all around the pattern pieces, trim to the cutting line.

Tip Use a rotary cutter to trim the units. It's neater and faster than scissors.

5. Join the separate units together. It's important that the pieces are joined accurately. Place a straight pin through the corners so they meet exactly and then pin the units together.

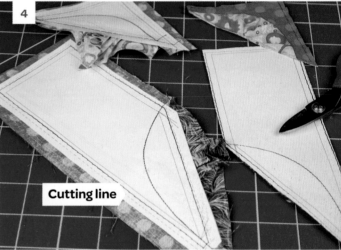

Cutting line

6. Sew the units together, giving you both a top and a bottom unit for each side of the panel. Press carefully, trying not to press the pleated sections flat. Trim the dog ears to reduce bulk.

7. Sew the two flower units together. Sew the left leaf, stem, and right leaf units together, pressing the seams open.

8. Continue to this point with the other two flower panels, using the dark fabric for the background. Sew the flower and leaf units together and press the seams open.

9. Add the two bands to the top and bottom of the flower panels. Stitch one band to the top of the panel and the other to the bottom edge.

Tear away the paper from the wrong side. Use tweezers to get the small scraps out of the corners.

## QUILT AND BIND

10. Follow the instructions on p. 14 to make a quilt sandwich. Quilt ⅛ in. around all the motifs in the flower panels and then echo the quilt stitching ½ in. away from the previous row. Continue echoing the previous row stitched until the background is filled. Quilt wavy lines in the top and bottom bands. Pull the beginning and ending quilting threads to the back side and tie into pairs with a square knot (see p. 11). Thread the ends into a large-eye needle, bury in the batting, and cut the ends so no threads show.

Trim the quilt to 16 in. square. If you are binding the quilt, make a continuous binding from the 2¼-in. strips of fabric. Then bind the quilt as instructed on p. 15.

## ADD THE YO-YOS

11. The yo-yo flowers are the final touch. With the flower fabric and pattern A, cut out three circles for the flower yo-yos. See p. 12 for directions for making yo-yos.

12. Tack the yo-yos in place with a needle and thread, making sure the top of the stem is covered.

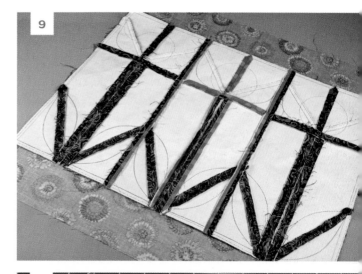

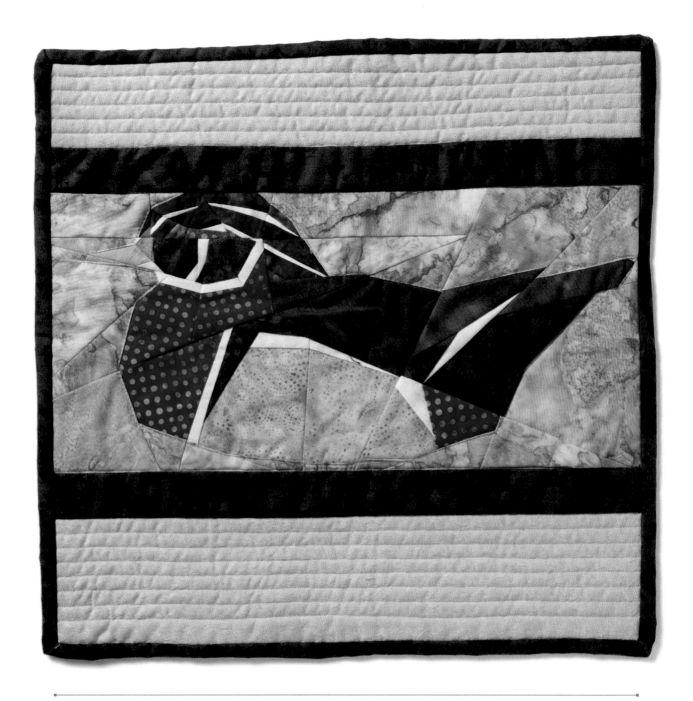

**THE DESIGN:** Paper piecing turns the impossible into the totally doable. Neither Jayne nor I would even think of piecing this project by cutting all those tiny shapes and sewing them together. The only difference between paper piecing and regular piecing is that there's a piece of paper on top with a nice, convenient line on which to sew.

You will need small pieces of fabrics for the paper-pieced portion this project. Batiks are a logical choice because they offer soft, strong colors and textures that mimic nature. Nothing beats a batik for a watery background.

# Paper-Pieced
# WOOD DUCK

DESIGNER: Jodie Davis

The wood duck is one of the most recognizable avians, and its colorful plumage makes for an eye-catching quilt. If you have done some paper piecing and are comfortable with it, forge ahead. You'll be pleased with the result!

SKILL LEVEL: Intermediate │ THE TECHNIQUE: Paper piecing (p. 91)

## What You'll Need

- Paper-Pieced Wood Duck template (pp. 164–166)
- Fabric scraps for the duck
- Fat quarter cream fabric for the top and bottom outer borders
- Fat eighth black fabric for the inner borders
- Fat quarter cream fabric for the backing
- ⅛ yd. black fabric for the binding
- 16½-in.-square batting
- Monofilament thread for quilting
- Newsprint or foundation paper made for paper piecing

## What You'll Learn

The only way to piece the duck's intricate coloring is with paper piecing, which can be a bit challenging. Try it and you'll be happy to have this in your skill set for tackling all sorts of situations in which precision and small pieces call for nothing else.

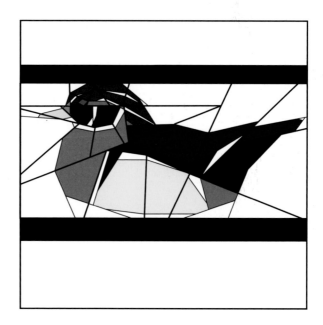

# Fabric Cutting Chart

Cut your fabrics according to this chart. When cutting scrap fabric for paper piecing, cut your fabric larger than the pattern pieces. Many of the patches for this project have funny angles, and large pieces give you lots of fudge room when lining them up.

| Piece | Measurements | No. of Pieces |
| --- | --- | --- |
| Top outer border | 16½" by 3" | 1 |
| Bottom outer border | 16½" by 4½" | 1 |
| Inner borders | 16½" by 1¾" | 2 |
| Backing | 16½" square | 1 |
| Binding | 2¼" by 42" to 45" | 2 |

## PAPER PIECE THE DUCK

1. Enlarging by 200 percent, copy the Paper-Pieced Wood Duck templates on pp. 164–166 and cut them out, leaving space outside of the cutting lines.

   Begin with block B. Place the wrong side of the fabric for patch 1 against the plain side of the paper, generously covering the area of patch 1. Remember that the printed side of the paper will be the wrong side of your quilt block. If you find it necessary, use a glue stick to hold it in place.

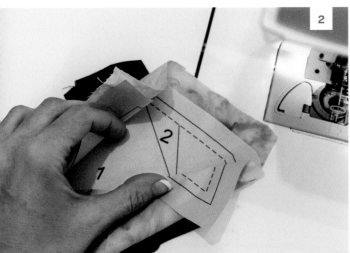

**Tip** Copy the layout for the entire wood duck (p. 83) and keep it by your sewing machine. You'll find it invaluable for keeping you on track as you piece the sections.

2. Lay your fabric for patch 2 on the sewing machine bed, right side up. Lay the patch 1 fabric on top, which just so happens to be glued to a piece of paper. (Remember it's the same as regular piecing—right sides together.)

3. Shorten the stitch length on your sewing machine to about 18 stitches per inch and sew the fabrics together, starting a few stitches before the line between patches 1 and 2 and ending a few after.

4. The pieces on the right side should look like photo 4.

5. Trim the seam allowances to about ¼ in. This doesn't need to be precise because as no one will see it.

6. Press patch 2 open.

7. As before, lay the fabric for the next piece, patch 3, right side up on the sewing machine bed and lay the block on top, fabric side down.

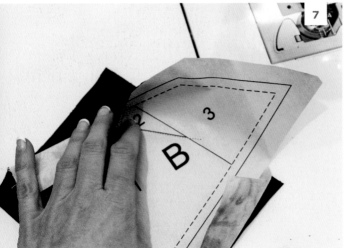

8. Stitch along the line between patch 2 and patch 3.

9. Trim the seam allowance and press patch 3 into place.

> **Tip** So that you don't have to always think about what goes where and in which direction when sewing, place the paper printed side up over the fabric for the next patch with the low number— the one you just sewed—to the left.

10. Once you have sewn all of the patches on block B, press it.

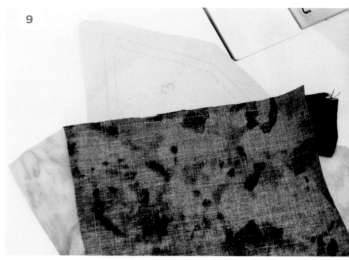

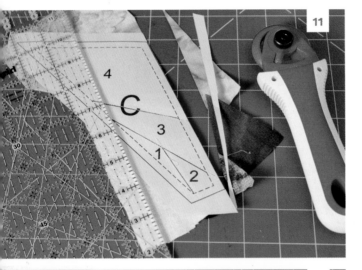

11. Trim along the solid outside lines. Repeat steps 1 to 12 to piece blocks A through T.

### JOIN THE BLOCKS

12. Sew the seams to join each block permanently. Start by joining block A to block B.

---

**NOTE:** Don't forget that the finished duck will be the mirror image of the pattern.

---

13. Join unit A–B to block C, then join that unit to block D.

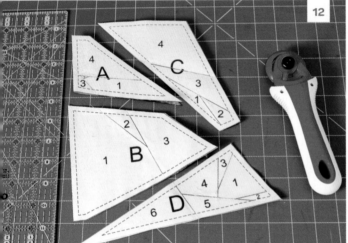

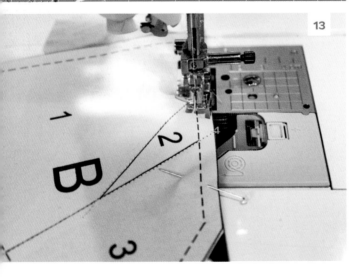

14. After sewing the seam between each block, remove the paper from the seam allowances only. This will help them press open or to the side nicely. Leave the rest of the paper attached until the quilt top is finished. The paper will hold everything steady until you stitch the blocks together, and as you will see farther along, when you join the blocks, the sewing lines on the paper make matching simple.

15. Press the seam.

16. When joined and turned right sides up, blocks A, B, C, D, and E should look like photo 16. You can see how the duck comes to life as you piece the blocks together.

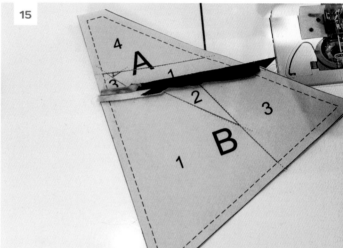

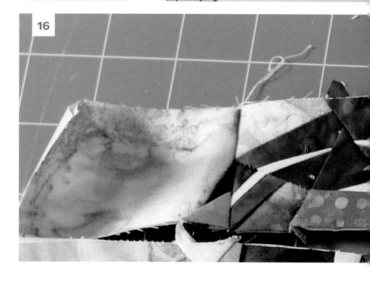

# Piecing the Duck Pattern

| Stitch This Block/Unit | To This Block Unit |
|---|---|
| E | F |
| E, F | F, G |
| E, F, G | H |
| I | J |
| K | L |
| I, J | K, L |
| I, J, K, L | M |
| I, J, K, L, M | N |
| I, J, K, L, M, N | O |
| P | Q |
| P, Q | R |
| P, Q, R | S |
| P, Q, R, S | T |
| P, Q, R, S, T | U |
| P, Q, R, S, T, U | I, J, K, L, M, N, O |
| I, J, K, L, M, N, O, P, Q, R, S, T, U | E, F, G, H |
| E, F, G, H, I, J, K, L, M, N, O, P, Q, R, S, T, U | A, B, C, D |

17. Continue piecing the blocks together as you did in steps 13 though 16, using "Piecing the Duck Pattern" at left as a guide. Press.

## ADD THE BORDERS

18. Stitch a black inner border strip to the long edge of each of the cream borders. Stitch the black strips to the long edges of the duck, with the wider border at the bottom.

## QUILT AND BIND

19. Tear the paper from your piecing. Follow the instructions on p. 14 to make a quilt sandwich. Stitch in the ditch above and below the black inner border strips. In the cream borders, use a presser foot as the width for the rows of stitching. Then stitch around the duck.

20. Trim the quilt to 16½ in. if necessary. If you are binding the quilt, make a continuous binding from the 2¼-in. strips of fabric. Then bind the quilt as instructed on p. 15.

## Piecing the Blocks

The stitching lines on the paper offer a fantastic guide for piecing the blocks together. The corners marked on the paper are easy to match up and result in perfect joins. Here's how:

- Place the two pieces you wish to join down, paper side up.
- Consult the block layout to make sure you are matching the correct edges. Pick the pieces up so the right sides are together.
- At one corner, push a straight pin into the corner of the blocks facing you, emerging straight out the fabric side of the block. Pin into the piece you wish to join on the fabric side and out at the corner marked on the paper. (It may take a few tries.)
- Repeat for the other end of the stitching line. Press the blocks together, pushing the pins in up to the heads. Place additional pins along the seam in the normal fashion to secure the blocks and remove your placement pins. Stitch.

**THE DESIGN:** To let the tucks shine, I kept this little quilt simple. Wavy pin tucks are made by folding fabric, stitching along the fold, and then stitching the resulting pleats so they fall into a wave. Each pleated square is constructed the same way, eliminating the need to keep track of which way to stitch the waves. By rotating the squares 90 degrees, the quilt attains a pinwheel effect thanks to the pleats.

# NIP AND TUCK

DESIGNER: Jodie Davis

Often found on blouses and children's clothing, pin tucks are decorative rows of stitched pleats. This technique offers quilters an easy way to add texture to their quilts. Of course, quilters don't stop with tucks. Stitching pleats in opposite directions, quilters have turned pin tucks into wavy pleats, as in this mini quilt.

---

SKILL LEVEL: Intermediate | THE TECHNIQUE: Fabric tucking (p. 94)

---

## What You'll Need

- ¼ yd. white fabric for the tucked squares
- ¼ yd. red fabric for the sashing
- ¼ yd. red fabric for the border
- Fat quarter cream fabric for the backing
- ¼ yd. red fabric for the binding
- 16½-in.-square or larger batting

## What You'll Learn

Bring a sense of movement and additional texture to fabric with wavy pin tucks. The techniques of folding and stitching the tucks can be applied to any project.

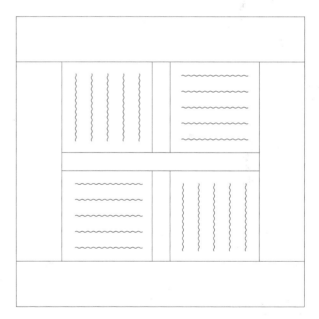

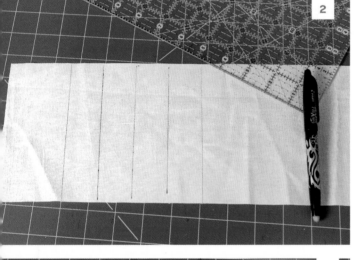

# Fabric Cutting Chart

Cut your fabrics according to this chart.

| Fabric | Measurements | No. of Pieces |
|---|---|---|
| Tucked squares | 5½" by 32" | 1 |
| Sashing | 1½" by 5½" | 1 |
| Sashing | 1½" by 11½" | 1 |
| Border | 3" by 11½" | 2 |
| Border | 3" by 16½" | 2 |
| Backing | 16½" square | 1 |
| Backing | 2¼" by 42" to 45" | 2 |

## MARK FABRIC FOR PIN TUCKING

1. Starting at the left edge of the 5½-in. white fabric, mark your first pin-tucking line 2½ in. from the left-hand edge.

---

**NOTE:** I used a heat-soluble marking pen. After I stitched the pleats into waves, I carefully held the iron above them to erase the lines without squishing the pleats.

---

2. Add four more lines, each 1¼ in. apart. Mark a line 3½ in. from your last line and then add four more lines, each 1¼ in. apart.

3. Add two more five-line groups as in step 2, marking the first line of the group 3½ in. from the last line. Repeat two more times.

---

**NOTE:** Rather than sew four different squares, it is easier to pleat a long strip and then cut it into sections. That way each square will come out the correct size. Each group of five lines is a pin-tuck section and will be separated after stitching.

---

4. On both long edges, mark a line 1 in. in from the raw edge.

## STITCH THE PIN TUCKS

5. Starting on the left side, fold the fabric along the first line. Stitch ¼ in. from the folded edge.

6. Repeat step 5 for all five lines, folding the fabric along the next line. Repeat for the next group of lines you marked.

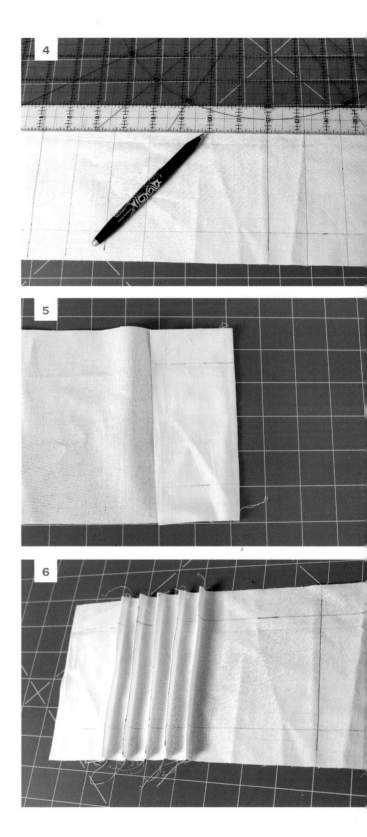

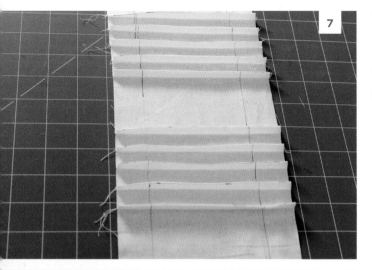

7. Repeat until all groups of lines have been stitched.

## CREATE THE WAVES

8. On one long side, stitch along the line you marked ½ in. from the raw edge using a regular stitch and folding the pleats flat as you sew. Be sure to fold all the pleats in the same direction.

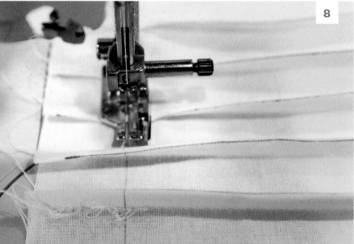

9. Turn the pleated strip in the opposite direction so you will start sewing on the short edge on which you just stopped sewing. Repeat step 9 on this side, pushing the pleats in the opposite direction to form the waves.

10. Press the sides of the pleats gently.

### CREATE FOUR TUCKED SECTIONS

11. Place your strip right side up and start working on the right-hand end. On one end of the strip, place the 1¼-in. line on the rotary ruler onto the right-most line of stitching. Trim away the extra fabric to the right of the ruler using a rotary cutter.

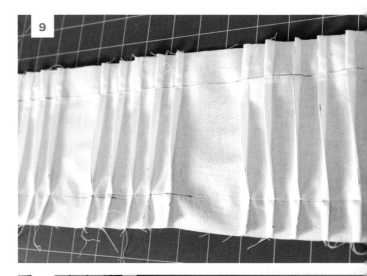

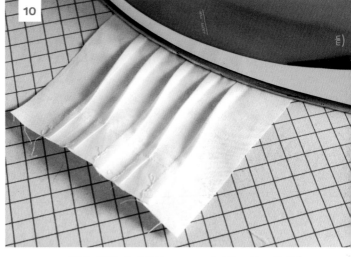

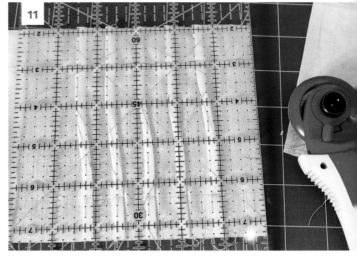

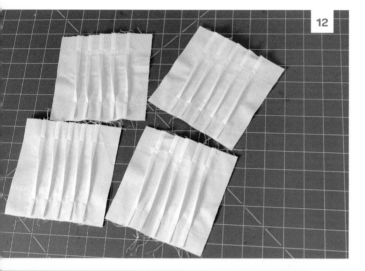

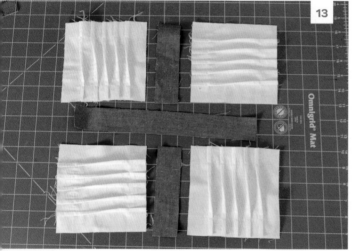

**12.** Repeat step 13 for all four sections until you have four separate tucked squares.

### ADD THE SASHING

**13.** Lay out the sashing as shown in photo 13, right side down, so the longer piece is horizontal in the center.

To achieve the pinwheel effect: Stack the pin-tucked squares right side down, so that all pleats are folded in the same direction. Place the stacked squares in one section. Pick the top three squares off the stack, rotate them 90 degrees counterclockwise, and place them in the next counterclockwise section. Repeat until all the squares have been laid out.

**14.** Stitch the short, vertical pieces of sashing to their corresponding tucked squares. Press the seams toward the sashing fabric.

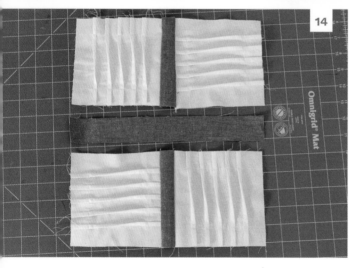

15. Stitch the long horizontal piece of sashing to one pair of squares.

16. Then stitch the horizontal piece of sashing to the other pair of squares. Press the seams toward the sashing.

## ADD THE BORDERS

17. Stitch the shorter border sections to the sides of the quilt. Press toward the sashing fabric.

18. Stitch the remaining border sections to the top and bottom edges of the quilt. Press toward the sashing fabric.

## TRIM, QUILT, AND BIND

19. Follow the instructions on p. 14 to make a quilt sandwich. To leave the border plain, simply quilt in the center of the sashing and in the ditch around the block of squares.

    Trim the quilt to 16½ in. if necessary. If you are binding the quilt, make a continuous binding from the 2¼-in. strips of fabric. Then bind the quilt as instructed on p. 15.

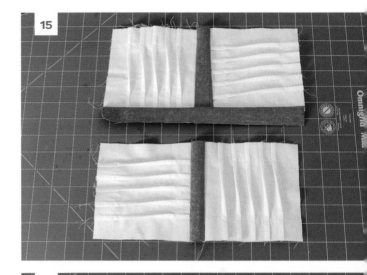

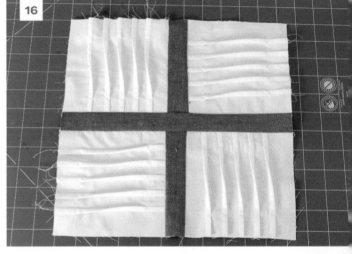

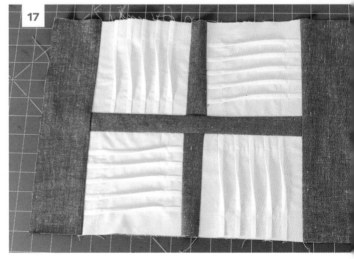

**THE DESIGN:** To accentuate the scallops, this quilt is put together using the pillowcase method rather than being layered into a quilt sandwich, quilted, and bound. The backing and quilt top are sewn right sides together on top of the batting, while the stitched and turned scallops are simply inserted into the seams of the quilt top as it is sewn together. Then the quilt is turned right side out and the seam is hand closed, eliminating the need for a binding.

# SCALLOPED!

DESIGNER: Jodie Davis

This quilt explores a very simple example of a design element you can use in your quilts as either a border or as three-dimensional texture. In this case, scallops are used both ways. The scallops are sewn, turned, and pressed and then inserted into the seams of the quilt top. Plus a row is stitched into the seam at the outside edges of the sides of the quilt.

SKILL LEVEL: Intermediate | THE TECHNIQUE: Inserted design element (p. 103)

## What You'll Need

- Scalloped! template on p. 156
- Fat eighth red fabric for the quilt top
- Fat eighth pink fabric for the quilt top
- ⅓ yd. cream fabric for the scallops
- Fat quarter fabric for the backing
- 14½-in. by 16½-in. batting
- Air- or water-dissolving pen
- Smoothly pointed turning tool (optional)

## What You'll Learn

For this design you will stitch scalloped strips, then insert them into the seams as you construct the quilt top. On p. 146 you'll see a beautiful throw using the same technique, but with a few tweaks to fit the larger size.

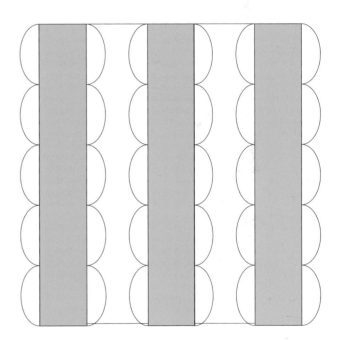

**NOTE:** The scallops on the sides of the quilt make it finish at 16 in. square.

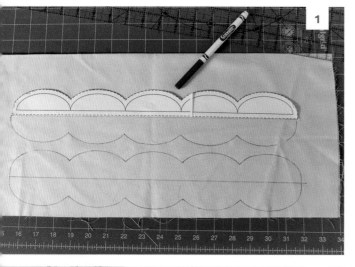

# Fabric Cutting Chart

Cut your fabrics according to this chart.

| Fabric | Measurements | No. of Pieces |
|--------|--------------|---------------|
| Red | 3" by 16½" | 3 |
| Pink | 3¾" by 16½" | 2 |
| Backing | 16½" by 14½" | 2 |

## TRACE THE SCALLOPS

1. Following instructions on p. 156, make three copies of the Scalloped! template and enlarge by 200 percent. Cut along the dashed lines. Tape the pattern together, omitting one scallop from the last template to form five scallops. Fold the cream fabric in half lengthwise. Lay the template on top of the doubled fabric and trace the scallops using an air- or water-dissolving pen. Trace another group of scallops, placing the template next to the first traced scallops to form a mirror image. Continue tracing until you have six groups of scallops.

## STITCH THE SCALLOPS

2. Beginning and ending with a backstitch, sew a strip of scallops along the curved edge using a ¼-in. seam allowance. Repeat for all six of the scallop pieces.

3. Cut along the straight line. Trim the seam allowance along the scalloped edges to about ⅛ in. Clip into the inside Vs up to the seam to help the curve lay flat when turned right side out. Do not clip past the seamline.

## FINISH THE SCALLOPS

4. Turn the scallop pieces right side out. For perfectly smooth curved edges, use a smoothly pointed turning tool to push the edges out from the inside. Run the tool along the seam a few times to push it all the way out, smoothing it into a perfect curve.

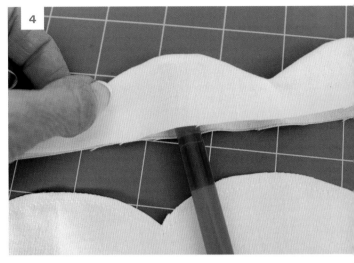

## SEW THE QUILT TOP

5. Match a scallop to one long edge of a right-side-up red strip. The scallop will stop short of the corners by ¼ in. Stitch the scallop in place along the length of the strip.

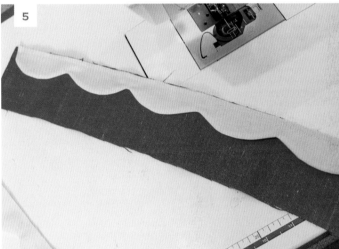

6. Match a scallop to the other edge of the red strip. Pin it in place.

### Get in Shape

In addition to scallops, you can insert folded triangles into seams. Or even simpler, folded strips of fabric. Quilters often use the latter as a way to add a second inside border to a quilt, which lends a small strip of color to bring out a color in one of the fabrics in the design. This type of edging can make a big difference in making a quilt sing.

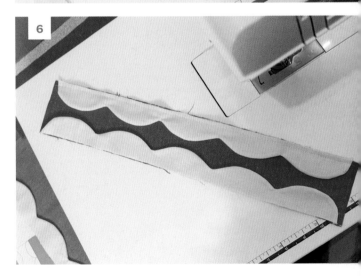

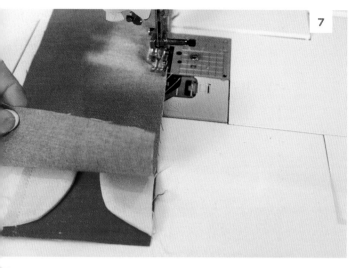

7. Place a pink strip on top, right side down, matching the raw edges of the strip you just finished.

8. Stitch the long edge of the pink strip to the scallop strip.

9. Place the straight edge of a scallop strip against the right-side edge of the pink strip. Place a red strip right side down on top of the scallop. The pink and red strips will be right sides together.

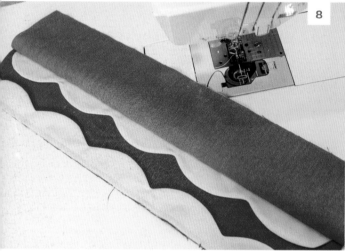

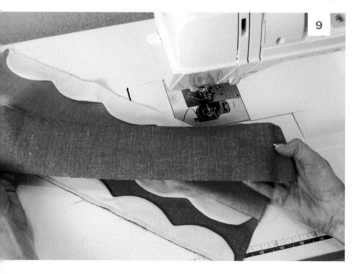

10. Sew the pink strip, scallop strip, and red strip together along the edge.

11. Repeat steps 6 to 10 until you have used all three red strips and both pink strips. Press the interior scallops toward the pink strips, leaving the two outside scallops folded in for now.

## LAYER AND STITCH THE QUILT

12. To eliminate the need for binding and to put the scallops center stage along the edge of the quilt, use the pillowcase method. Here's how.

    Place the batting on your work surface. Place the quilt top right side up on top of the batting. Place the quilt backing right side down on the quilt top, matching the edges. Pin the layers in place along the edges.

    Beginning with a backstitch, stitch about 4 in. from a top or bottom edge—one without the scallops. Continue around until you turn the fourth corner. Stitch about 4 in. from that corner, leaving a 4-in. to 6-in. opening. Backstitch.

    Trim the seam allowances close to the seam at the corners of the quilt to reduce the bulk.

    Turn the quilt right side out. Use a pointed tool to push the corners out neatly. Hand-stitch the opening closed.

## QUILT

13. Using a 3.5 to 4.0 machine stitch, stitch the red strips in vertical rows ½ in. apart.

    Trace the scallops onto the pink fabric below them. Stitch ½ in. away from the marking to outline the scallops.

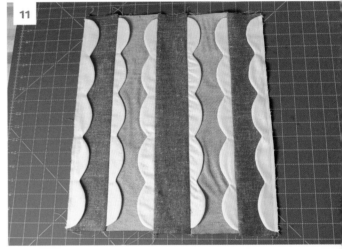

THE DESIGN: The fun of this project is you can do as little or as much as you like; adding the photo personalizes the quilt. Choose an old photo or a current one of someone you love or use a photo of your pet, a beautiful landscape, or a wonderful vacation spot. If you want even more embellishment, add beads, buttons, laces, colorful silk or velvet ribbons, silk ribbon embroidery—whatever suits your fancy.

# Today's
# CRAZY QUILT

DESIGNER: Jayne Davis

Traditionally, crazy quilts were made in silks and velvets and were a riot of embellishment with lots of handwork. I wanted a more updated, less labor intensive version. And then I found the perfect embellishment. I was going through some old family photos and came across a charming picture of three little girls taken in about 1880. The youngest girl, on the left, is my uncle Dick's mother, Grace, with her two sisters. I love the look of the modern crazy quilt with the vintage photo.

---

SKILL LEVEL: Intermediate | THE TECHNIQUES: Using your home printer to create templates (p. 108), printing on fabric (p. 110)

---

## What You'll Need

- Today's Crazy Quilt templates and pattern on p. 167
- Photograph
- 5 fat quarters coordinating batik fabrics in beiges and browns
- ⅔ yd. contrasting turquoise batik for the binding and backing
- 1 sheet prepared fabric for printing such as EQ Printables Premium Cotton Lawn Inkjet Fabric sheets
- 17-in.-square batting
- 18-in. square fusible web such as Lite Steam-A-Seam2
- Four yards ⅜-in. dark brown grosgrain ribbon
- Pinking shears
- Four 8½-in. by 11-in. sheets plain newsprint for templates
- Two 8½-in. by 11-in. sheets freezer paper for templates

## What You'll Learn

Making a crazy quilt is like working a puzzle to make all the pieces fit together. You'll end up with a mini quilt that highlights the pieces using ribbon bands. You'll also learn how to print a photo of your choice onto prepared fabric.

# Fabric Cutting Chart

Cut your fabric according to this chart.

| Fabric | Measurements | No. of Pieces |
|---|---|---|
| Turquoise binding | 2¼" by 42" to 45" | 2 |
| Backing | 17" square | 1 |

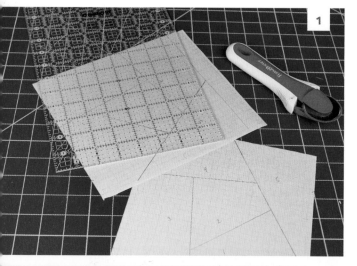

## MAKE THE QUILT BLOCKS

1. To make the four 8-in-square blocks, first copy the Today's Crazy Quilt Layout pattern on p. 167 and enlarge it by 400 percent. This is your layout sheet.

   Place the newsprint sheets in your printer paper tray and print four copies of the layout pattern—one per sheet.

   Copy the Today's Crazy Quilt templates pieces on p. 167 and enlarge 200 percent.

   Place the freezer paper sheets in the paper tray so they will print on the dull side of the paper. Print one copy of each pattern page.

2. Use a see-through ruler and a rotary cutter that you use for paper to trim the pattern pieces on the lines. These are your templates for cutting the crazy quilt pieces.

   Press a template very lightly onto the fabric. It will adhere, making it very easy to cut around with your see-through ruler and rotary cutter. The freezer paper template is reusable, so pull it off when finished, apply it to another section of fabric, and press it again. Cut four pieces in the same fabric for each pattern piece.

3. Assemble the pieces for a block following the layout sheet you copied earlier. Place pieces 1 and 2 in. their proper places with the joining edges butted together rather than on top of one another. Zigzag-stitch over the edges to join the pieces.

Add piece 3, and zigzag-stitch it to pieces 1 and 2. Continue with pieces 4 and 5 to complete one block.

Repeat this step to make the other three blocks.

## ATTACH THE RIBBONS

4. Refer to the ribbon layout drawing at right to apply the ribbons to cover all the raw edges. Attach in the order shown on p. 167 so all ribbon ends are covered.

5. Stitch down each side of the ribbon with a straight stitch, stitching as close to the edge of the ribbon as possible.

> **Tip** Most sewing machines allow the quilter to move the needle position to the left and right of center. Moving the needle can allow you to stitch closer to the edge of the ribbon Practice first on a scrap. Be sure you're using an open-toe foot so the needle won't hit the foot and break.

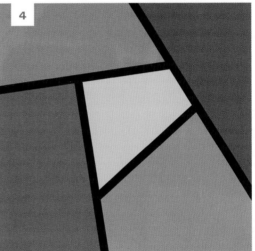

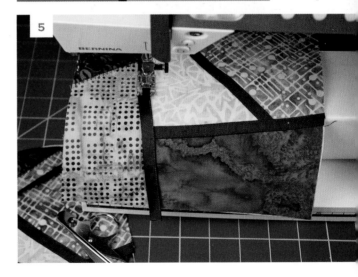

## JOIN THE QUILT BLOCKS

6. Join the blocks (two over two) using a zigzag stitch. Cover the two long seams with ribbon. Tear away the paper backing behind the crazy quilt pieces. Don't worry about the paper under the ribbon.

## PRINT AND APPLY THE PHOTOGRAPH

7. Print your photograph onto the fabric following the manufacturer's directions.

   Apply fusible web to the back of the printed photo and trim it to size. Use pinking shears to pink around the edges.

   Cut the photo backing fabric, making it ½ in. larger all around than the printed photo.

   Finger press the fusible web onto the back of the coordinating fabric, following the manufacture's directions. Pink all the edges.

## QUILT AND BIND

8. Follow the instructions on p. 14 to make a quilt sandwich. Attach a walking foot to your machine and quilt right up next to all the ribbon pieces.

9. Fuse the backing fabric onto the quilt following the manufacturer's instructions. Then center the photograph on the backing fabric and fuse.

10. Stitch around both the backing and photo close to the pinked edge. Trim the quilt to 16 in. square. If you are binding the quilt, make a continuous binding from the 2¼-in. strips of fabric. Then bind the quilt as instructed on p. 15.

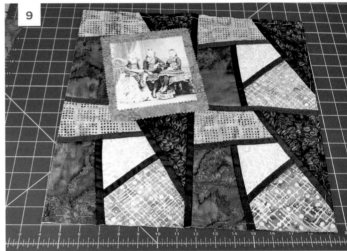

**THE DESIGN:** Trapunto is applicable to many designs. Whether lending three dimensions to an object, such as a piece of fruit, or to vines and geometric motifs, the technique is fun to play with. This piece uses both a simple linear lineup of straight rows of stitches and an overall pattern involving straight lines and curves that looks like the orange peel design. The asymmetry adds to the visual interest and puts the two different stitching designs center stage.

# TRAPUNTO-ESQUE

DESIGNER: Jodie Davis

Have you seen those exquisite whole-cloth quilts with gorgeous stuffed motifs that pop from the quilt top? This is achieved by a handwork technique called *trapunto*. The raised areas are quilted and then stuffed. Our mini quilt project is a pseudo-trapunto piece, taking its cue from some of my guests on *Quilt It! The Longarm Quilting Show*. To achieve this look, many guests use two layers of batting, including an 80/20 cotton/poly on top for added pouf. By stitching closely in some sections, the more open areas puff up, à la trapunto. It's faster and easier than the traditional method and offers a similar effect.

**SKILL LEVEL:** Intermediate  |  **THE TECHNIQUE:** Pseudo-trapunto (p. 115)

## What You'll Need

- Trapunto-esque template (p. 159)
- Fat eighth white fabric for the trapunto sections
- ½ yd. red fabric for the trapunto sections and borders
- ¾ yd. fabric for the backing
- ¼ yd. red fabric for the binding
- Two 20-in.-square or larger battings, preferably a wool blend for loft
- Newsprint or freezer paper for templates

## What You'll Learn

To make this easier version of the fancy-looking trapunto technique, you'll machine-quilt through two layers of batting.

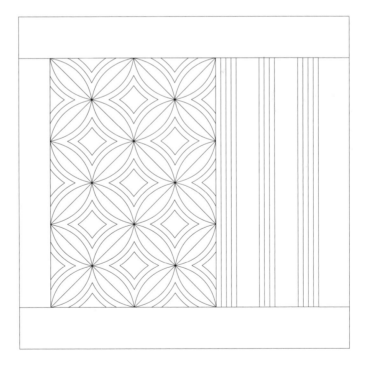

# Fabric Cutting Chart

Cut your fabrics according to this chart.

| Fabric | Measurements | No. of Pieces |
|---|---|---|
| Backing | 20" square | 1 |
| White trapunto | 10" by 15" | 1 |
| Red trapunto | 7" by 15" | 1 |
| Red side borders | 2" by 12½" | 2 |
| Red top and bottom borders | 2½" by 16½" | 2 |
| Binding | 2¼" by 42" to 45" | 2 |

**NOTE:** The fabrics for the trapunto sections are cut larger than the finished size to allow room in which to work.

## PREPARE FOR QUILTING

1. Make a quilt sandwich by placing the backing fabric wrong side up on a table. Place the two layers of batting on top. Safety pin the outer edges together.

   Position the white trapunto fabric on top so it is centered top and bottom and so the left-hand edge is about 3 in. from the left-hand edge of the batting. Place the red trapunto piece on top, aligning the right-hand edges. Stitch along the edge of the red fabric through all layers of the quilt sandwich.

2. Open the red fabric to the right. Using a long basting stitch, baste the left edge of the white fabric and the right edge of the red fabric through all layers to secure while you are quilting.

3. Copy the Trapunto-esque template on p. 159 and enlarge it by 400 percent. Print or copy the pattern onto the newsprint and cut it out.

Lightly glue-stick the pattern to the fabric square. Keep the overlap of the pattern sections to a minimum to make removing the paper easier. Matching the line on the pattern between the two sections of quilting with the seam that you just sewed, use basting spray or pins to secure the pattern to the quilt top.

---

**NOTE:** The edges of the paper are the seamlines between the trapunto sections and the borders.

---

## QUILT

4. Quilt the straight lines in the red section using a short stitch length, stopping and starting off the paper. There is no reason to secure the ends of this stitching because they will be secured when you stitch the border.

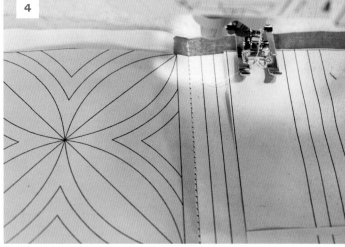

**Tip** Err on the side of a shorter stitch length for your quilting. Tearing the paper away after you quilt will stress your stitches; the shorter they are, the better they will withstand the tugging.

5. Stitch the straight lines of the orange peel pattern.

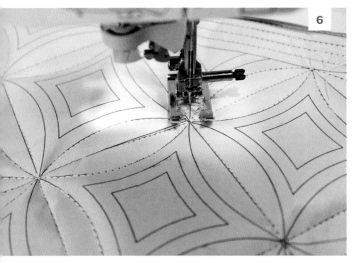

6. Starting at one corner, stitch the winding orange peel curves in the white fabric section. By going from one side of one oval to the opposite side of the next oval, you will be able to stitch most of the pattern without stopping. For easier tying later, be sure to leave long thread tails where you start and stop on the edge adjoining the red fabric and for the interior triangles. For the other three edges, start and end a few stitches off the paper.

7. Stitch the inner curves of the square shapes.

### ADD THE BORDER

8. On one long edge of a 2-in.-wide red border strip, mark a line ¼ in. from the raw edge. Place the strip on top of a side edge of the red trapunto section. Align the marked line with the edge of the paper.

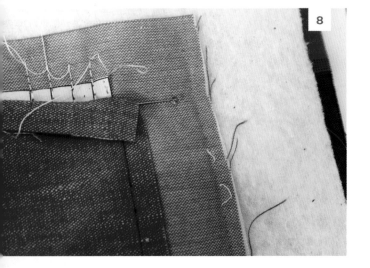

9. Using a 2.0 stitch length, stitch the seam. Press the seam open. Repeat for the other side.

10. Add the top and bottom borders as you did for the side borders.

11. Tie the thread tails together at the back of the quilt for the interior triangles and along the seam between the red and the white fabrics. Remove the paper by gently tearing it away from your stitching. A seam ripper is helpful in getting the tiny places and for scoring the paper to help it release more easily.

## TRIM AND BIND

12. Trim the quilt to 16½ in. square. If you are binding the quilt, make a continuous binding from the 2¼-in. strips of fabric. Then bind the quilt as instructed on p. 15.

THE DESIGN: Because I wanted to make a 16-in. mini quilt, the design had to be scaled down a bit from the vintage version. Lots of quilters are afraid of the idea of appliqué, thinking that it's too hard or takes too long. I've eliminated those excuses, making it easy by using fusibles and a sewing machine.

# Historic Appliqué
# GONE MODERN

DESIGNER: Jayne Davis

I love the look of appliqué, especially the big, bold designs and bright colors in some 19th-century quilts. A common color combination in those days was bright yellow, red, and green, and I decided that trio couldn't be improved on. The blocks in vintage quilts were huge, up to 36 in. square, making the appliqués easy to work. I've sized them down for this design, but the impact is still just as strong.

---

SKILL LEVEL: Intermediate │ THE TECHNIQUES: Window appliqué pieces (p. 120), blanket stitch (p. 122)

---

## What You'll Need

- Historic Appliqué Gone Modern templates on p. 159
- ½ yd. yellow fabric (A) for the background and backing
- ¼ yd. green fabric (B) for the leaves, stems, and binding
- Fat quarter red fabric (C) for the flower
- Scrap light red fabric (D) for the flower centers
- 18-in.-square batting
- Fusible web
- Matching threads for the appliqué

## What You'll Learn

I'll show you how to "window" the appliqué pieces to reduce the bulk and give you helpful hints for machine blanket stitching. To create a tabletop cover from this design, see p. 150.

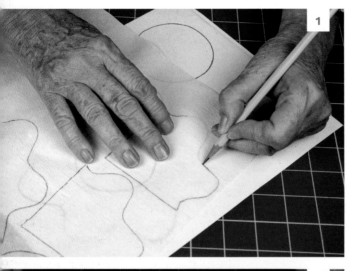

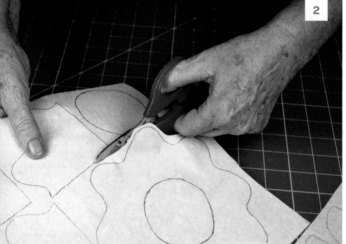

# Fabric Cutting Chart

Cut your fabrics according to this chart.

| Fabric | Measurements | No. of Pieces |
| --- | --- | --- |
| Background (A) | 16" square | 1 |
| Backing (A) | 18" square | 1 |
| Binding (B) | 2¼" by 42" | 2 |

## PREPARE THE PATTERN

1. Enlarge the Historic Appliqué Gone Modern templates on p. 159 by 200 percent. Following the manufacturer's directions for fusible web, trace the templates on the web. The number of pieces to trace is marked on each template.

   Cut a piece of 2-in. by 8-in. fusible web for the stems.

2. Roughly cut out the pattern pieces traced on the fusible web. (You will cut on the marked line later.)

3. Reduce the bulk of the larger pieces using a technique called *windowing*. Cut out the center of each of the rose pattern pieces to within ½ in. of the outline.

> **Tip** When pressing the appliqué pieces in place, use an up and down motion. See the tip on p. 9 for more on the difference between pressing and ironing.

4. Following the manufacturer's directions, press the pattern pieces onto the wrong side of the proper fabric: leaves on fabric B, the rose on fabric C, and the rose center on fabric D. Now you are ready to cut out each piece, carefully following the outlines. You will have 8 leaves, 1 full rose, 1 full rose center, 4 quarter roses, and 4 quarter rose centers.

5. Press the fusible web you cut for the stems onto the wrong side of fabric B. Cut along the edges of the web, and then cut the resulting rectangle into four ½-in. by 8-in. pieces.

## APPLY THE APPLIQUÉS

6. Place your clear ruler diagonally from corner to corner on the background fabric, ¼ in. from the exact corner. This helps you place the stems. Remove the paper backing, exposing the glue, from one stem piece. Place it 2 in. above the corner along the edge of the ruler. Repeat for the other three corners. (Make sure the rose pieces will cover the ends of the stems.) Press in place.

Add the four corner rose pieces, the center rose (make sure it's in the exact center) and rose centers. Press well.

Arrange the leaves last, referring to the photograph on p. 118. Finger press them in place and rearrange if needed, before using an iron to fuse the leaves. Note that each leaf sits exactly opposite its partner on each side of the stem and this same position repeats on each stem. You want the tips of the leaf ends to face each other around the whole block, making a quasi-circle.

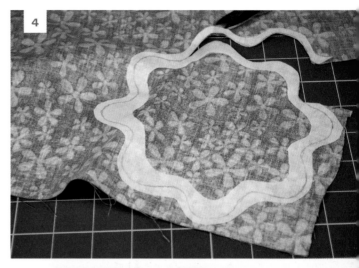

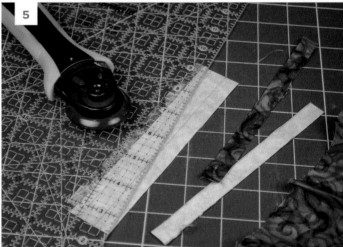

APPLIQUÉ

7. Many sewing machines have decorative stitches, and most include a blanket stitch (sometimes called a buttonhole stitch). Check your machine's manual for any necessary setup and instructions. Practice on scrap fabric to get the stitch length and width that please you (I used a length of 2.5 and width of 3) and so you'll know exactly where the needle will be in each part of the stitch. Stitch slowly so you can turn as you work around the gentle curves. Use thread that matches each piece of the appliqué design for the stitching.

Pull your beginning and ending threads to the back side, knot, and clip.

**NOTE:** If your machine doesn't have a blanket stitch, you still have options. You could stitch a straight line very close to the edge or you could hand-embroider the blanket stitch, which goes quickly and looks very nice. See p. 75 for instructions.

## QUILT

**8.** Follow the instructions on p. 14 to make a quilt sandwich. Quilt your design using a thread that matches the background. Use the same color thread in the bobbin. Stitch ⅛ in. outside all the appliqué pieces, outlining the design. Echo quilt, stitching ½ in. from the previous row.

## TRIM AND BIND

**9.** Pull all the beginning and ending quilting threads to the back side. Tie pairs together in a square knot (see p. 11) and thread them into a large-eyed needle. Bury the threads in the batting for an inch or so and trim off.

Trim the block to 16 in. square. If you are binding the quilt, make a continuous binding from the 2¼-in. strips of fabric. Then bind the quilt as instructed on p. 15.

> **Tip** When stitching the blanket stitch, turn your fabric when the needle is to the right in the stitch position. If you turn when the needle is in the "bite" position of the stitch, it will make an untidy V in the stitch.

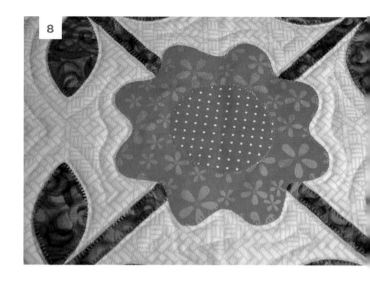

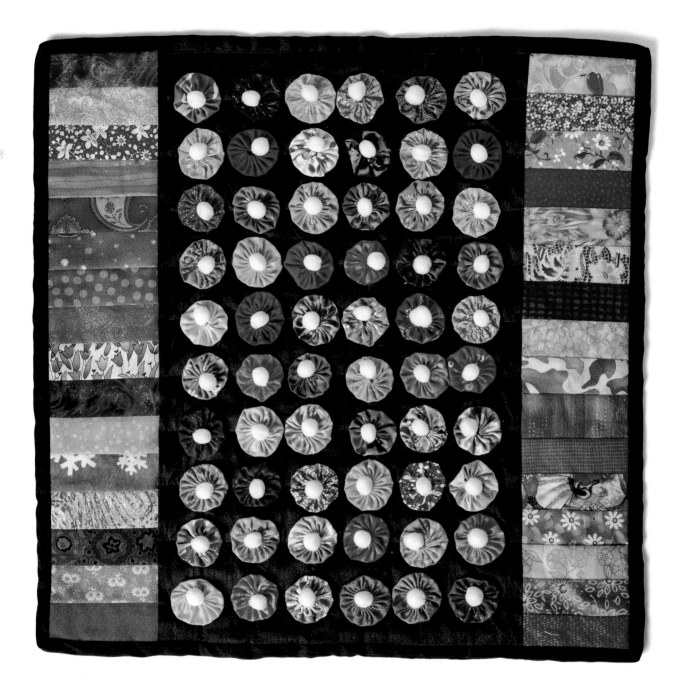

**THE DESIGN:** It's funny how designs evolve. This one started as a circle, but the image of rows of yo-yos with scrappy strips of colorful, stacked logs became irresistible. I chose silk for the black background behind the yo-yos and for the binding. The shininess of the silk sets off the yo-yos and makes the little quilt even more special. Another great choice for background fabric would be regular cotton quilting fabric.

# YO-YO QUILT

DESIGNER: Jodie Davis

Yo-yos exude charm. They are fun to make and a great take-along hand project. There's something about gathering flat circles into pretty little domed, gathered yo-yos that is immensely satisfying as you work. It's relaxing handwork, and the result is so satisfying.

SKILL LEVEL: Easy │ THE TECHNIQUE: Making yo-yos (p. 12)

## What You'll Need

- Yo-Yo Quilt template on p. 161
- Scraps from each of 60 different fabrics
- 1½-in. by 3-in. rectangles from each of 32 different fabrics for the side sections
- Fat eighth black silk for the background
- Fat quarter fabric for the backing
- ¼ yd. black fabric for the binding
- 16½-in.-square batting
- Black thread for quilting
- Sixty 10mm or ¼-in. white pompoms
- File folder for template
- Nonpermanent fabric marker

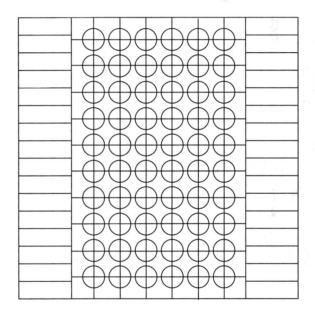

## What You'll Learn

Learn to make yo-yos, and you'll soon discover why they have been popular for generations. And you'll be hooked on them!

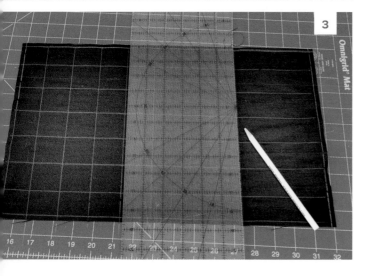

# Fabric Cutting Chart

Cut your fabric according to this chart.

| Fabric | Measurements | No. of Pieces |
|---|---|---|
| Black background | 10½" by 16½" | 1 |
| Backing | 16½" square | 1 |
| Black binding | 2¼" by 42" to 45" | 2 |

## PIECE THE SCRAPPY SIDES

1. Arrange the rectangles into two rows, each 16 rectangles tall. Rearrange until the colors suit you. Stitch the rectangles into two rows.

2. Press seam allowances in one direction.

> **Tip** A gridded pressing pad is helpful when pressing pieced strips. Use a straight line to ensure that you are pressing the pieced units into straight strips.

## MARK THE BACKGROUND

3. Draw lines 1½ in. apart lengthwise on the right side of the black silk fabric. Repeat going along the shorter side.

4. Continue marking until you've completed the entire grid. Mark a ¼ in. line along the row edges to designate the seam allowance.

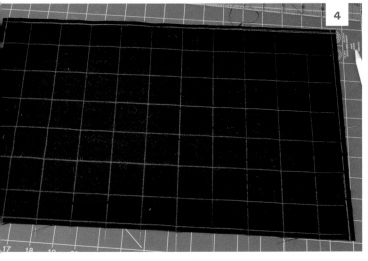

## CONSTRUCT THE QUILT TOP

5. Stitch the side panels to the marked silk background.

6. Press the seam allowances toward the center.

## LAYER, QUILT, AND BIND

7. Follow the instructions on p. 14 to make a quilt sandwich. Using the quilting thread and a long stitch—3.5 works well—stitch along the grid lines from raw edge to raw edge.

   Trim the quilt to 16½ in. if necessary. If you are binding the quilt, make a continuous binding from the 2¼-in. strips of fabric. Then bind the quilt as instructed on p. 15.

## PREPARE THE YO-YOS

8. Copy the Yo-Yo Quilt template on p. 161. Trace the pattern onto scrap fabric. You should have 60 circles when you are finished cutting.

## STITCH THE YO-YOS

9. The most efficient way to make this quilt is to make each yo-yo and, instead of clipping the thread and going on to make another, stitch the yo-yo to the quilt top right then and there. It saves time rethreading.

   Follow the instructions on p. 12 to make the yo-yos.

10. Make a knot to close your stitching, but do not cut the thread.

## APPLY THE YO-YOS AND POMPOMS

11. With your thread still attached, sew the yo-yo at an intersection of two quilting lines, gathered side up, catching the center of the yo-yo just outside the gathers. This will be covered by the pompom, so don't fuss over it too much. Now, come up through the yo-yo and run the needle through the middle of the pompom. Go back down through the yo-yo.

12. Knot at the back of the quilt. Repeat for all of the yo-yos, being mindful of color placement.

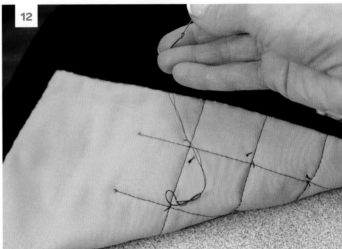

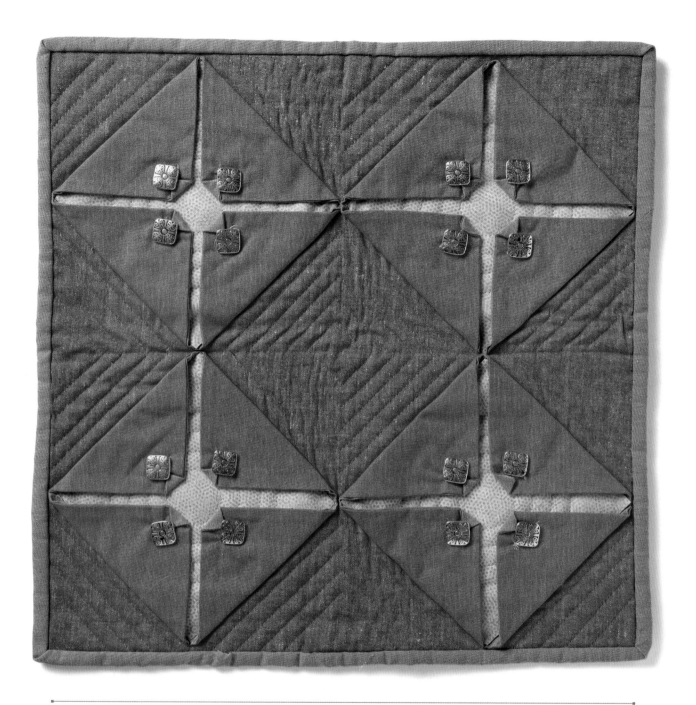

THE DESIGN: Fabric folding can be complex, borrowing techniques from origami or those used in a cathedral window quilt, a tried-and-true traditional favorite. My mini quilt is of the simpler persuasion. But don't be fooled, simple can still be quite dramatic!

# 3-D SQUARE-IN-A-SQUARE

DESIGNER: Jodie Davis

Intended for a wall instead of a bed, mini quilts offer the opportunity to play with some techniques that wouldn't be appropriate for sleeping under. Fabric folding is a good example. My design for this mini is a simple square, the corners folded to the inside and then the tips folded out and held in place with a fancy bead. The idea here is not to fold and hold everything down flat, rather to let the folded fabric pop from the quilt top to celebrate the texture. This is a play on the very common and exceedingly useful square-in-a-square block.

SKILL LEVEL: Intermediate | THE TECHNIQUE: Fabric folding (p. 133)

## What You'll Need

- 3-D Square-in-a-Square template on p. 158
- Fat quarter red fabric for the quilt top
- ¼ yd. green fabric for the folded squares
- ¼ yd. orange fabric for the folded squares
- ¼ yd. yellow fabric for the centers of the squares
- Fat quarter fabric for the backing
- ¼ yd. green fabric for the binding
- 16½-in.-square or larger batting
- Fusible web such as Steam-A-Seam2
- 16 beads or buttons
- Air- or water-dissolving pen
- Newsprint or freezer paper for template
- Smoothly pointed turning tool

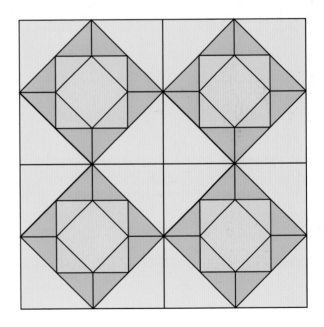

## What You'll Learn

A simple fabric folding technique adds texture to the quilt. A stitched-and-turned, two-sided fabric square is stitched to the quilt top and folded for a three-dimensional effect.

# Fabric Cutting Chart

Cut your fabrics according to this chart.

| Fabric | Measurements | No. of Pieces |
| --- | --- | --- |
| Green | 8½" square | 4 |
| Orange | 8½" square | 4 |
| Yellow | 26" by 6½" | 1 |
| Fusible web | 26" by 6½" | 1 |
| Red | 16½" square | 1 |
| Backing | 16½" square | 1 |
| Binding | 2¼" by 42" to 45" | 2 |

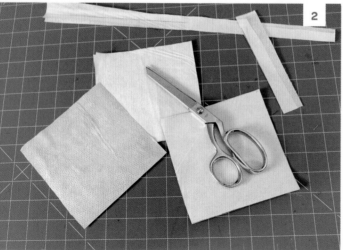

## STITCH THE SQUARES

1. Make a slash in the center of an orange square. Place a green and orange square right sides together. Stitch all the way around using a ¼-in. seam allowance. Trim the seam allowances at the corners to reduce bulk. (This will be covered by the yellow square later.) Turn right sides out. Push the corners of the square out using a smoothly pointed turning tool. Press.

## ADD THE YELLOW CENTERS

2. Following the manufacturer's instructions, apply the fusible web to the wrong side of the piece of yellow fabric. Using a rotary cutter and ruler, cut it into four 5½-in. squares.

3. Remove the paper from the fusible web and place it right side down on top of the green fabric. Fuse.

## PREPARE, LAYER, AND QUILT

4. With the 16½-in. square of red fabric, mark the quilt top for placement of the squares by folding it in half and in half again. Press or use a marker to mark the folds.

   Follow the instructions on p. 14 to make a quilt sandwich.

   Using the lines on the red quilt top for guidance, place a stitched square on the top, yellow side up, matching two edges of the square to the folded lines on the quilt top. There will be ¼ in. of quilt top extending past the square at both outside edges. Using a stitch length of 3.0, stitch the square to the quilt through all layers, stitching along the edge of the yellow square.

5. Stitch around the entire yellow square.

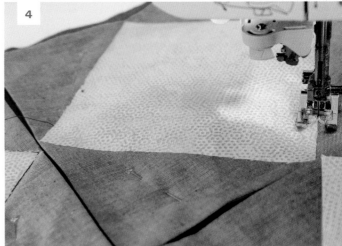

6. Repeat for all of the squares. The squares' edges will touch at the center of the quilt.

7. Using a 3.5 to 4.0 machine stitch, quilt the red squares in rows. Start by quilting a square inside the outside edge of the square. Repeat five times. Use the edge of your presser foot as a guide or use the quilting guide that came with your machine.

> Tip  To quilt the squares, I used the quilting guide for my sewing machine set at ½ in.

8. Enlarging by 200 percent, copy the 3-D Square-in-a-Square template on p. 158 onto newsprint or freezer paper. Place the template on a yellow square. Use basting spray or simply hold it in place. Quilt the circles. Tear the paper away.

## BIND AND FINISH

9. If you are binding the quilt, make a continuous binding from the 2¼-in. strips of fabric. Then bind the quilt as instructed on p. 15.

Fold the three-dimensional triangles to the inside of the yellow squares, positioning them so that the triangles are raised on the quilt a bit rather than lying flat. Pin. Stitch a bead or button, using the finished quilt photo on p. 130 as a guide. Fold the tip of the triangle back and tack in place with a few stitches, just under the bead or button.

# 3

## MINI QUILT PROJECTS

# Made for Minis

Mini quilts lend themselves to being turned into all manner of items. Pillows are a natural. Keep them 16 in. square as we have done for several of the designs or add a border to make it larger. Freshening up a room or changing its personality is as simple as swapping out a set of pillows. In fact, I used this book as an opportunity to revamp both my bedroom and den with the new designs.

The fun doesn't stop there! You can make totes or a hobo bag to show off your mini beauties. You can stitch three minis together to create a table runner, or if the design is conducive, make them one piece as in the Stenciled Table Runner project on p. 153.

Of course, there is always the possibility of a quilt. When you make one mini quilt top and fall for the technique, go ahead and make more and soon you'll have a throw or even an entire quilt for your bed.

These projects are so fun, you'll quickly be joining me in being mad for minis!

# Picky Piecing
# MODERN GRAPHIC TOTE BAG

**DESIGNER:**
Jayne Davis

I was trying to think of good things to make from these mini quilts when the light bulb in my head clicked on: Make a tote bag. The Picky Piecing Modern Graphic Quilt design (p. 24) can be turned into a smashing tote. To make this bag, I made two minis and used different color fabrics.

## What You'll Need

- 1 yd. light-colored batik fabric (A) for the wide strips
- Fat quarter medium-colored fabric (B) for the pieced strips and top edge binding
- Fat quarter dark-colored fabric (C) for the pieced strips
- Scrap bright-colored fabric (D) for highlights in the pieced strips
- ½ yd. contrasting fabric for backing (which becomes the bag's lining)

---

**NOTE:** The quantities are different from the mini quilt on p. 24 because you will make two minis for the tote bag.

---

- Two 21-in. by 20-in. battings
- 2 yd. webbing for the handles (in color to match fabrics)
- 6-in. by 10-in. sheet poster board for shaping the tote
- Seam roll or tightly rolled up towel

## MAKE THE TOTE BAG

1. Make two mini quilts (without binding) as shown on p. 24, using the ½ yd. contrasting fabric as backing. Do not bind the quilt top.

2. Cut two 2¼-in. by 20-in. strips from fabric B for the top binding. Join to make a continuous binding strip (see p. 15) and press in half, wrong sides together.

   Using your favorite seam-finishing machine stitch, stitch all around both mini quilts. A regular zigzag stitch also works just fine. If this isn't available on your machine, whipstitch all the edges by hand.

   With right sides together, join the bottom edges of the two minis, matching the stripes. Pin in place and stitch with a ¼-in. seam.

> **Tip** When using a zigzag stitch, do not stitch over the edge because this will cause the edge to tunnel.

3. Press the seam open using seam roll.

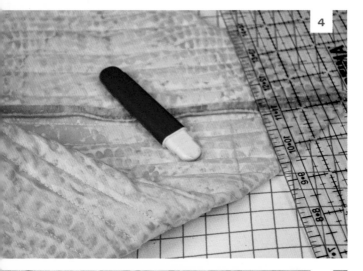

4. With right sides together, join the side seams, pin, and machine stitch.

   Press the side seams open.

   To make the flat bottom of the bag, fold in the bottom edge on each side to make a triangle shape. Mark a seam 3 in. down from the tip of the triangle. Machine stitch across the marked line.

5. Fold the triangles toward the center of the bag's bottom seam and hand-tack in place.

6. Turn the tote right side out. Prepare to add the binding for the top edge of the bag. Open the binding. Fold and finger press ½ in. along one edge to the inside. Refold the binding.

   Along the top edge of the bag, place the raw edges of the bag and the turned-under edge of the binding together, right sides facing, and pin in place. Overlap the ends of the binding by 1 in. and cut off rest of the binding. Machine stitch a ¼-in. seam.

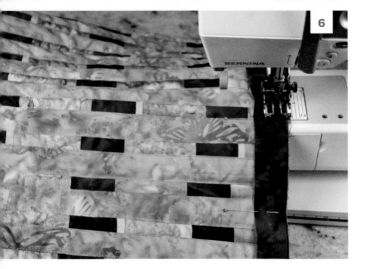

7. Turn the binding to the lining side and slipstitch the folded edge into place.

8. Cut the webbing into two 28-in. pieces and machine finish the ends.

    Measure 4½ in. in from each side seam near the top edge of both the front and back. Fold back 1 in. of each end of the webbing. Pin both ends of one piece of webbing to each side of the 4½-in. marks, being sure not to catch the binding.

9. Machine-stitch the handles in place, making a 1-in. square on the webbing. Do not stitch into the binding.

    Place the piece of poster board in the bottom of the bag so it will hold its shape. For a more finished look, you can wrap the poster board with an 8-in. by 12-in. piece of the lining fabric as if you were wrapping a package; secure in place with fabric glue before inserting the board in the bag.

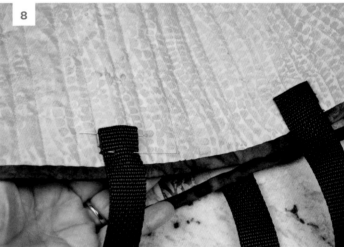

# Mini
# QUILT PILLOW

DESIGNER:
Jayne Davis

The size alone dictates that these mini quilts are perfect candidates for pillows. For my own home, I made pillows using the All Tied Up in Wool pattern (p. 68). For her home, Jodie made pillows using the Hawaiian Gone Modern Stenciled Quilt (p. 54) and the Decorative Stitched Circles pattern (p. 34). Use the pattern that works best for your design needs.

## What You'll Need

- **All Tied Up in Wool (p. 68) pattern or mini quilt pattern of your choice**
- **18-in.-square muslin for the quilt backing**
- **16½-in.-square fabric for the pillow backing**
- **16-in.-square pillow form**
- **Handful of polyester stuffing**
- **Seam roll or tightly rolled up towel**

## MAKE THE QUILT PILLOW

1. Follow the mini quilt directions on p. 68 through tying the quilt together in step 5. Use the muslin square as the backing for the quilt sandwich and do not apply the binding.

   Trim the quilt sandwich to 16½ in. square after tying.

2. Layer the quilt top and pillow backing, right sides together. Match the raw edges.

   Pin together, leaving a wide opening at the bottom to insert the pillow form. Machine-stitch, rounding the corners. The rounded corners will make the pillow look better when finished.

   Turn the pillow cover inside out and carefully press it using a seam roll.

3. Fill the four corners tightly with polyester stuffing. Insert the pillow form. Pin the opening at the bottom edge and slipstitch closed.

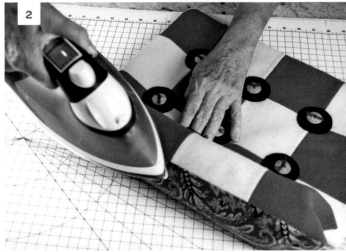

# Scalloped!
# THROW QUILT

DESIGNER:
Jayne Davis

I really liked the Scalloped! mini quilt (on p. 100) Jodie designed, and I decided this idea would make a knock-out 42-in. by 60-in. throw quilt. With the other projects made from the mini quilts we've stayed within the 16-in. square format. But for the throw I wanted to maintain the flow of the scallops across the entire piece. That required a bit of a change in construction techniques.

## What You'll Need

- Scalloped! template (p. 156)
- 3¼ yd. dark turquoise batik fabric for the narrow rows and backing
- 1¼ yd. light turquoise batik fabric for the wide rows
- 2½ yd. fuchsia batik fabric for the scallops and binding
- 44-in. by 64-in. batting
- Three 8½-in. by 11-in. sheets freezer paper for the templates
- Adhesive tape

## MAKE THE THROW

1. Place the freezer paper in the copier so the dull side will be printed on. Enlarge the Scalloped! template on p. 156 to 200 percent. Make six copies, each printed onto the freezer paper.

   Cut out the pieces of the pattern along the dotted line and tape them together, making sure the tape is on the dull side. You'll end up with a template 21½ in. long.

2. Fold the fuchsia fabric in half lengthwise. Fold it in half again so the top and bottom raw edges are together. You now have four layers of fabric. Trim a straight edge.

   Place the scallop template shiny side down with the bottom edge on the fabric's raw edges. Press lightly with a dry iron to adhere it to the fabric. Mark along the scallop edge with a marking pen. This will be the cutting line for the scallops.

   Using a 24-in. see-through ruler and rotary cutter, cut 2 in. below the raw edge to separate the row.

3. Remove the template. Pin the layers of the cut row together, making sure they do not shift. Carefully cut along the marked line. The four layers of fabric yield two 42-in.-long pieces, which will be the front and back of one scallop row.

   Press the template on the raw edge once more and repeat steps 2 and 3 until you have cut 10 rows.

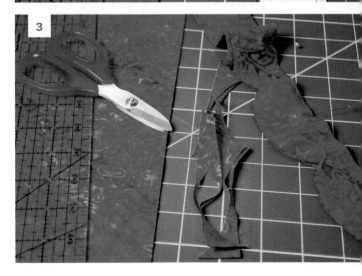

4. From the remaining fuchsia fabric, cut six pieces 42 in. to 44 in. (depending on the width of your fabric) by 2¼ in. for the binding.

   Fold the light turquoise fabric in half lengthwise. Cut a straight edge across the raw edge. Cut 10 pieces across the width of the fabric, each 3¾ in. wide.

5. From the dark turquoise fabric, cut a length 65 in. long. This will be the quilt backing.

   Fold the remaining dark turquoise fabric in half lengthwise. Cut 11 pieces across the width of the fabric each 3 in. wide.

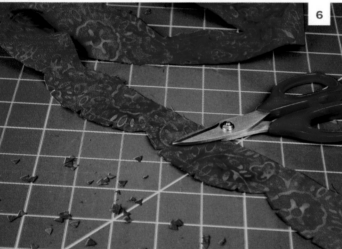

6. Open a pair of cut scallops. Pin them with right sides together. Stitch ¼ in. from the cut edge, carefully following the curves. Make several V-shaped clips along each scallop, making sure you do not clip into the seamline. This will give the strip a sharper edge when it's turned inside out.

## ASSEMBLE THE QUILT

7. Turn the scallops inside out and press. Repeat for all 10 scallop rows.

   Begin with a narrow dark turquoise row, right side up. Top it with a scallop row, with the raw edges together. Add a wide light turquoise row right side down and raw edge matching the other two. Stitch in a ¼ in. seam. Open and press the seam toward the dark fabric.

8. Top the light turquoise strip with a scallop row and a dark turquoise row. Stitch and press the seam toward the dark fabric. Continue until you've used all the cut rows, ending with a dark turquoise row.

9. Press well. Follow the directions on p. 14 to make a quilt sandwich. Quilt straight rows in both the light and the dark fabrics.

10. Trim the quilt to square up the edges. Make a continuous binding from the 2¼-in. strips of fuchsia fabric. Then bind the quilt as instructed on p. 15.

# Historic
# APPLIQUÉ TABLE TOPPER

DESIGNER:
Jayne Davis

The 16-in. Historic Appliqué Gone Modern mini (p. 118) was designed with a future in mind. When four or more of these blocks are joined together, a beautiful all-over Rambling Rose design pops up. For this project, I joined four blocks together and added two borders. The result is a cheerful 40-in.-square table topper. Add more squares and you'll have a larger tablecloth or a bright throw. Add enough squares and you can have a king-size bed quilt. Just remember: you're working in 16-in.-square increments.

## What You'll Need

- 2½ yd. blue batik fabric (A) for the background and backing
- ⅔ yd. green fabric (B) for the leaves, stems, borders, and binding
- ⅔ yd. red fabric (C) for the flowers, quarter flowers, and borders
- Fat quarter light red fabric (D) for the flower centers
- 44-in.-square batting
- Fusible web such as Lite Steam-A-Seam2

**NOTE:** The fabric quantities are different from the Historic Appliqué Gone Modern quilt on p. 118 because you'll make four minis for the table topper; plus you'll need fabrics for the borders and additional binding.

## MAKE THE TABLE TOPPER

1. From fabric A, cut four 16½-in. squares. The remaining fabric will be your backing fabric.

   From fabric B, cut four 2¼-in. by 42-in. to 44-in. strips across the width of the fabric for the binding. Cut four 1½-in. by 36-in. pieces for the inside borders.

   From fabric C, cut four 3½-in. by 42-in. to 44-in. pieces across the width of the fabric for the outside borders.

   Make four Historic Appliqué Gone Modern mini quilts as directed on p. 118. Stop after appliquéing all the design pieces in step 7. Trim to 16½ in. square.

2. Pin two mini quilt blocks together, carefully matching the designs. Sew together using a ¼-in. seam and press the seam open. Repeat with the other two blocks. Then sew these units together, forming a two-block by two-block square.

> **Tip** There's a reason for trimming the border pieces to the exact measurements. It is, of course, faster to just stitch on the borders and trim off the excess. But this very often results in a wavy edge, and no amount of pressing or wishing will make the borders lie flat.

3. Press the quilt top and trim if necessary to 32½ in. square.

Take two of the 1½-in. strips of fabric B for the inside border and trim to 32½ in. long. Sew them along opposite sides of the square and press the seams toward the border.

Measure the width of the block plus the two attached inside borders. Your quilt top should be 34 in. Trim the remaining inside border pieces to that length and sew the strips along the other two sides.

Add the outside borders, using the 3½-in. strips of fabric C, following the same directions. Measure, trim, stitch, and press the borders for the first two sides. Then measure, trim, stitch, and press the remaining borders.

## QUILT AND BIND

4. Follow the direction on p. 14 to make a quilt sandwich. Attach a walking foot to your sewing machine and quilt your quilt. I outline stitched the appliqué and stitched four wavy lines in the outer borders. It is not an easy task to fold and turn a quilt this size on a home sewing machine, but it certainly can be done.

Trim away the excess batting and backing fabric. Square up your quilt.

Make a continuous binding from the 2¼-in. strips of fabric B. Then bind the quilt as instructed on p. 15.

# Stenciled
# TABLE RUNNER

**DESIGNER:**
Jodie Davis

Personalize your dining table with a stenciled table runner. This is the only project that doesn't use a mini quilt you already made. Instead it uses the mini quilt technique. To make the table runner, you may use the stencil from the mini quilt project on p. 54, picking colors to match your décor. Or you can create your own stencil by lifting a design element from your room such as a motif from your dinnerware.

## What You'll Need

- **1 yd. yellow fabric for the top of the table runner and backing**
- **¼ yd. beige fabric for the binding**
- **17½-in. by 39½-in. batting**
- **5 colors of acrylic paint**
- **Stencil plastic or recycled file folders**
- **Stencil brush, natural sponge, or special stencil applicator**
- **Embroidery floss**

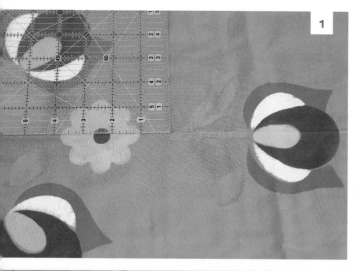

## STENCIL AND STITCH THE QUILT TOP

1. Cut a 16½-in. by 38½-in. rectangle from the yellow fabric for the top of the table runner. Cut a 17½-in. by 39½-in. rectangle from the yellow fabric for the backing.

   Follow the instructions for the Hawaiian Gone Modern Stenciled Quilt on p. 54 to prepare your stencils. Stencil the motif at the center of the runner, placing the stencil so the yellow flower runs along the long center line. Then add a tulip along both long ends, 1 in. from the yellow flowers.

2. Stencil a yellow flower ¾ in. from the tip of the tulip on each long end.

## QUILT AND BIND

3. Follow the directions on p. 14 to make a quilt sandwich. Work a running stitch with the embroidery floss around the design elements, as instructed on p. 57.

   To trim the ends of the runner at an angle, position the 45-degree line of your ruler along one raw edge. Slide it toward or away from the corner, adjusting it until the corner of the ruler at zero is at one edge and the 8-in. marking is at other.

4. Cut along the ruler's edge. Repeat for the other three corners.

5. Cut four 2¼-in. by 42-in. to 45-in. (depending on the width of your fabric) strips from the beige fabric. Bind the quilt as instructed on p. 15.

6. Bind the corners in the usual manner, stopping ¼ in. from the corner and backstitching, then turning your work and pulling the binding tail up so it is folded and its raw edge is an extension of the raw edge of the quilt.

7. Fold down the binding strip so it aligns with the raw edge of the quilt.

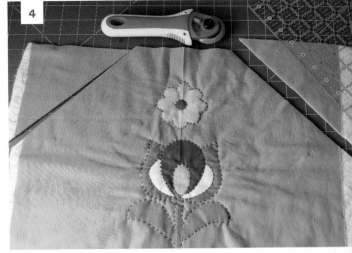

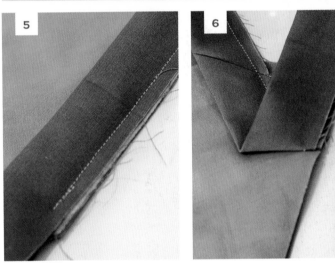

# TEMPLATES

## DECORATIVE STITCHED CIRCLES

Enlarge the template by 400 percent, one-quarter of the pattern at a time. Tape the pattern together.

## SCALLOPED!

For the mini quilt, enlarge the template by 200 percent and make three copies. Cut along the dashed lines. Overlap and tape them together to make a pattern with five scallops.

For the throw quilt on p. 146, enlarge the template by 200 percent and make six copies. Tape together to make a template that is 21½ in. long.

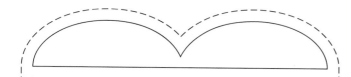

## ALL TIED UP IN WOOL

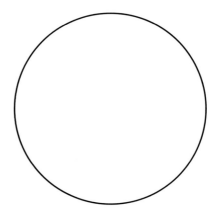

# IN THE JUNGLE

Copy the templates. Enlarge the templates by 200 percent. Join the four pieces where marked, attaching A to B and so on.

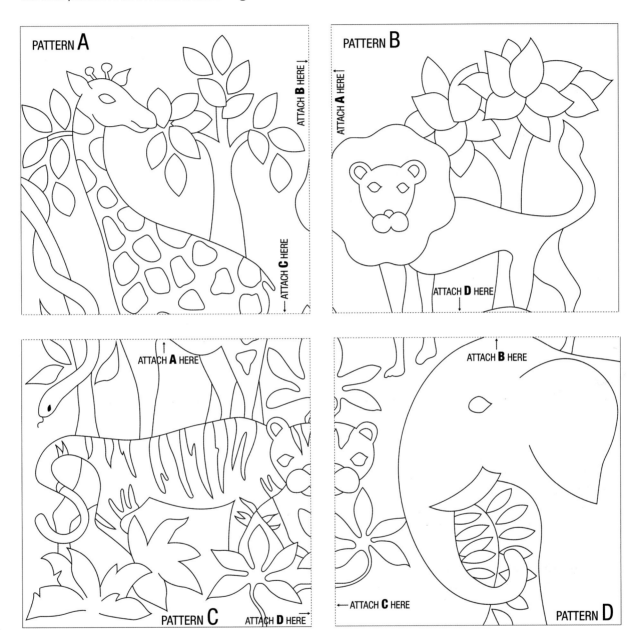

PATTERN A — ATTACH B HERE — ATTACH C HERE

PATTERN B — ATTACH A HERE — ATTACH D HERE

PATTERN C — ATTACH A HERE — ATTACH D HERE

PATTERN D — ATTACH B HERE — ATTACH C HERE

## HAWAIIAN GONE MODERN STENCILED QUILT

Enlarge the red flower template by 400 percent and the yellow flower template by 200 percent.

### Red Flower

Cut a separate stencil for each color.

Place along pressed foldline

Place along pressed foldline

Center of block

### Yellow Flower

## FRAYED STAR

Enlarge the templates by 400 percent.

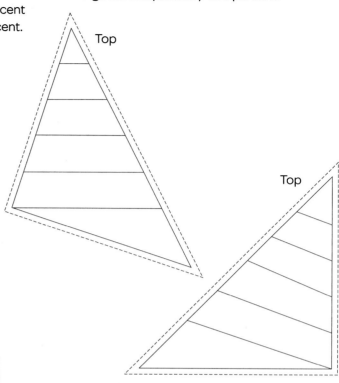

Top

Top

## 3-D SQUARE-IN-A-SQUARE

Enlarge by 200 percent.

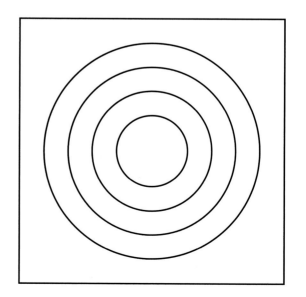

## TRAPUNTO-ESQUE

Enlarge the templates by 400 percent.

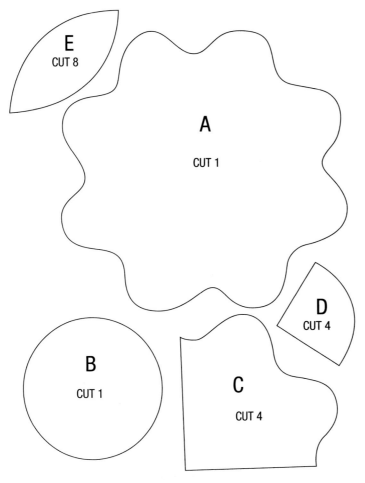

E
CUT 8

A
CUT 1

## HISTORIC APPLIQUÉ GONE MODERN

Enlarge the templates by 200 percent.

D
CUT 4

B
CUT 1

C
CUT 4

# SWEDISH FOLK ART IN FELT

Copy the templates as directed and enlarge the pattern by 200 percent.

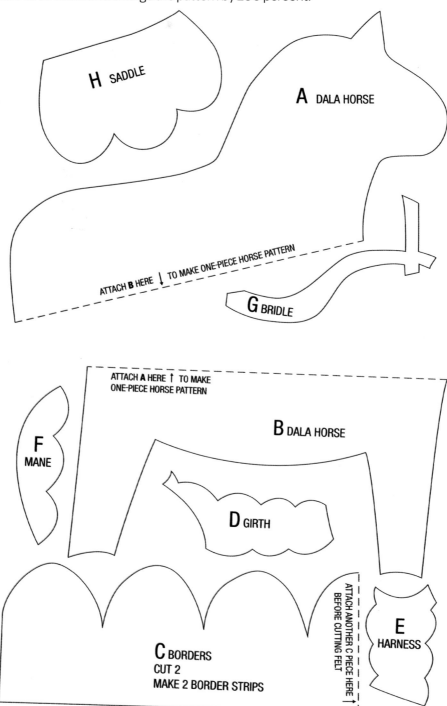

ATTACH **B** HERE ↓ TO MAKE ONE-PIECE HORSE PATTERN

**H** SADDLE

**A** DALA HORSE

**G** BRIDLE

ATTACH **A** HERE ↑ TO MAKE
ONE-PIECE HORSE PATTERN

**F** MANE

**B** DALA HORSE

**D** GIRTH

**C** BORDERS
CUT 2
MAKE 2 BORDER STRIPS

ATTACH ANOTHER C PIECE HERE
BEFORE CUTTING FELT

**E** HARNESS

## HORSE SILHOUETTE

Enlarge the template by 200 percent.

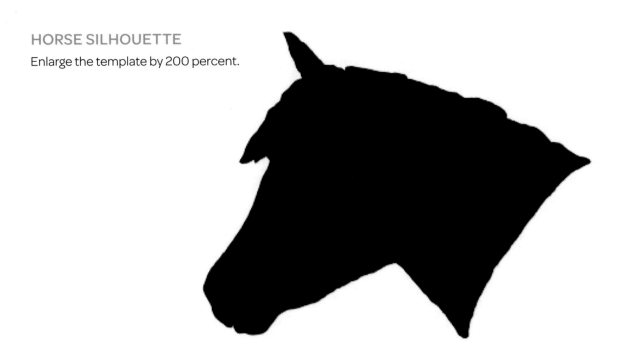

## THREAD PAINTING

Enlarge the template by
300 percent.

## YO-YO QUILT

3 inch circle. Make 60.

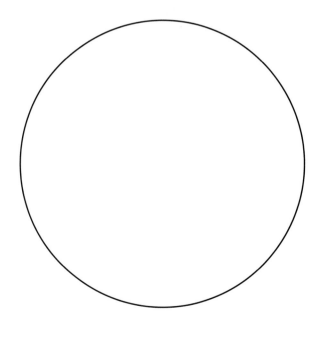

## ARTS AND CRAFTS FLOWERS

Enlarge these templates by 200 percent and print three copies of each onto newsprint.

NOTE: The dotted line is the cutting line, and the solid line is the stitching line. Roughly cut the pieces apart, cutting outside the dotted line and working one flower panel at a time.

**Diagram**

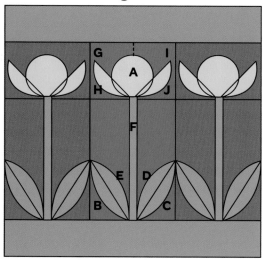

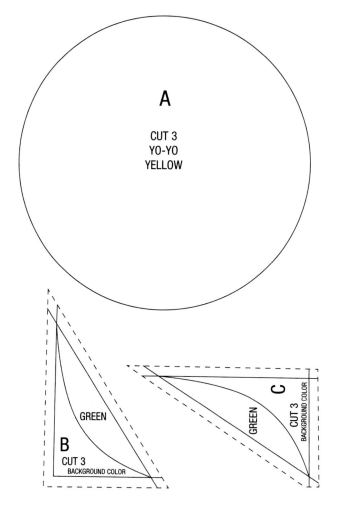

**A**

CUT 3
YO-YO
YELLOW

**B**
GREEN
CUT 3
BACKGROUND COLOR

**C**
GREEN
CUT 3
BACKGROUND COLOR

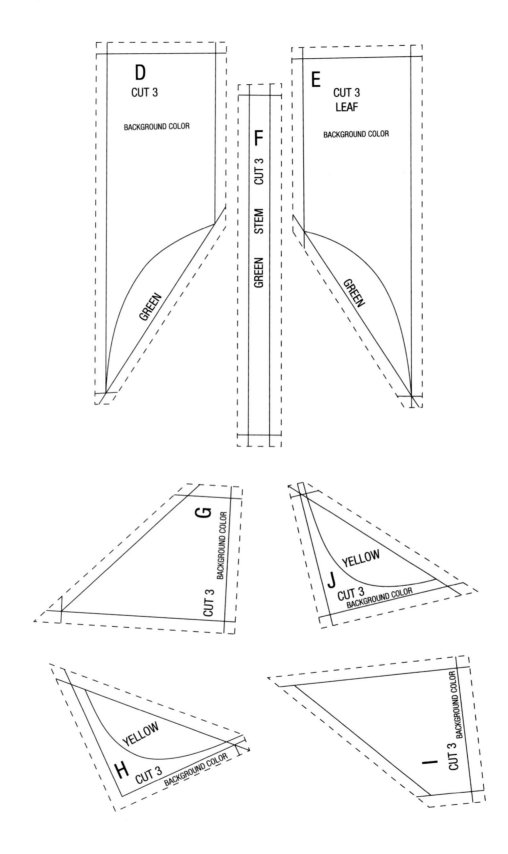

# PAPER-PIECED WOOD DUCK

Enlarging by 200 percent, copy the templates and cut them out, leaving space outside of the cutting lines.

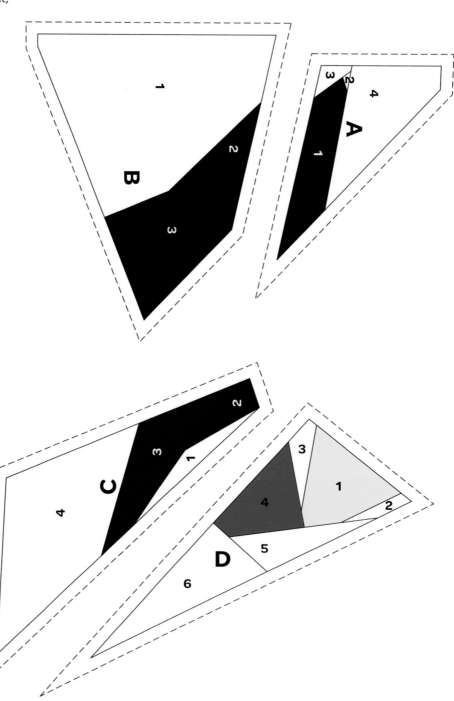

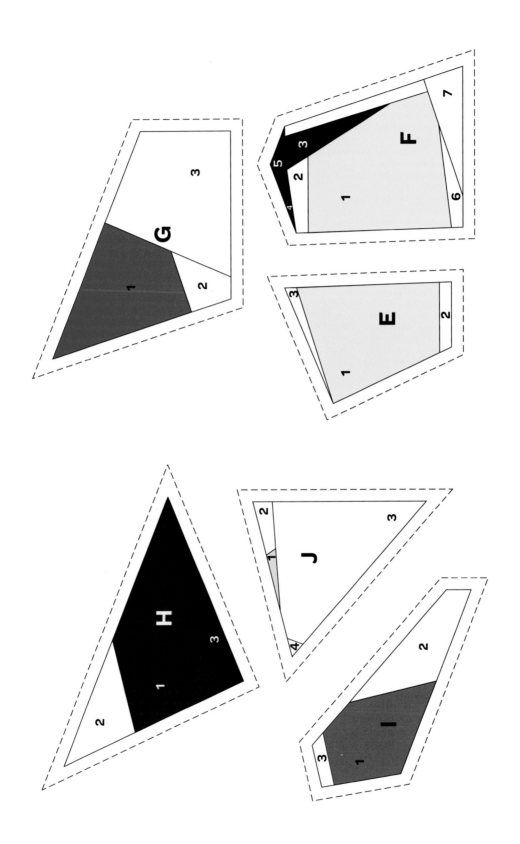

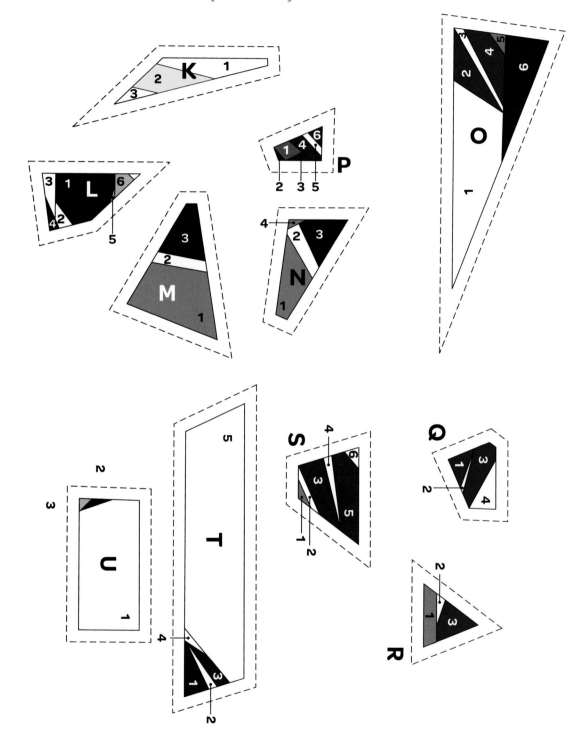

## Templates

Enlarge by 200 percent.

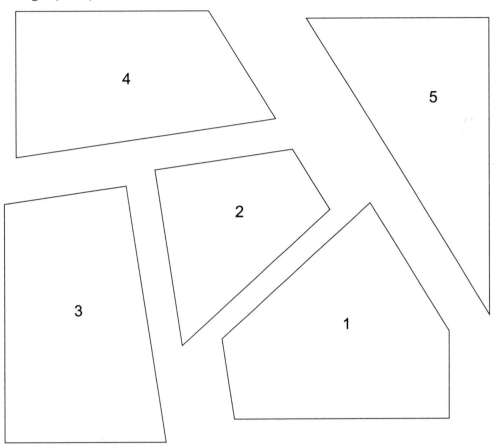

## Layout pattern

Enlarge layout pattern by 400 percent.

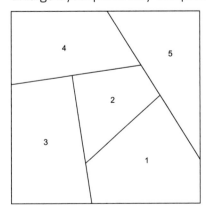

## Ribbon layout

Enlarge layout pattern by 400 percent.

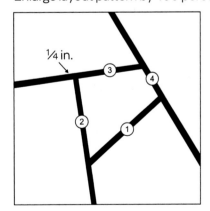

¼ in.

# METRIC EQUIVALENTS

**One inch equals approximately 2.54 centimeters. To convert inches to centimeters, multiply the figure in inches by 2.54 and round off to the nearest half centimeter, or use the chart below, in which figures are rounded off (1 centimeter equals 10 millimeters).**

| | | |
|---|---|---|
| ⅛ in. = 3mm | 4 in. = 10cm | 16 in. = 40.5cm |
| ¼ in. = 6mm | 5 in. = 12.5cm | 18 in. = 45.5cm |
| ⅜ in. = 1cm | 6 in. = 15cm | 20 in. = 51cm |
| ½ in. = 1.3cm | 7 in. = 18cm | 21 in. = 53.5cm |
| ⅝ in. = 1.5cm | 8 in. = 20.5cm | 22 in. = 56cm |
| ¾ in. = 2cm | 9 in. = 23cm | 24 in. = 61cm |
| ⅞ in. = 2.2cm | 10 in. = 25.5cm | 25 in. = 63.5cm |
| 1 in. = 2.5cm | 12 in. = 30.5cm | 36 in. = 92cm |
| 2 in. = 5cm | 14 in. = 35.5cm | 45 in. = 114.5cm |
| 3 in. = 7.5cm | 15 in. = 38cm | 60 in. = 152cm |

# GLOSSARY

Like the any craft, quilting sometimes requires lingo you may not be familiar with. Here are a few words and terms that I use throughout the book.

### BACKSTITCH

A method to secure your stitching at either the beginning or the end of your stitching. It's actually just sewing backward for a few stitches, then continuing forward, making sure to stay on the seamline.

### DOG EARS

The little triangles that extend past the corner of a quilt block when seam allowances are opened away from each other. Clipping these away eliminates bulk.

### ECHO QUILTING

A sewing technique that can be done by machine or by hand. A design is outlined with stitching and then repeated at uniform distances, echoing the shape of the motif and allowing it to stand out.

### FAT EIGHTH

A cut that is 9 in. by half the width of the fabric. No shops in my neck of the woods sell fat eighths, but maybe they do in your area.

### FAT QUARTER

A regular quarter yard is 9 in. by the width of the fabric. A fat quarter is 18 in. by half the width of the fabric.

### FREE-MOTION QUILTING

A technique in which the quilt is moved as the quilter turns curves. Turn the work as you stitch without putting the needle down.

### FUSIBLE WEB

A two-sided adhesive that bonds two surfaces (usually fabrics) together. We used Steam-A-Seam2 and Lite Steam-A-Seam2 in several of the mini quilt projects.

### SASHING

Strips of fabric between quilt blocks to frame the blocks. Sometimes *cornerstones* are added, which are little squares that meet at the corners of the sashing.

### STITCH IN THE DITCH

Stitching directly into the seamline. Your stitching should not skip up onto the visible fabric. Stitch slowly for best results. This technique is used when quilting the layers together.

### TOPSTITCH

A technique in which a line of stitching is sewn on top of a seam or near an edge to give a finished look.

# RESOURCES

Visit these websites for additional information about quilting and the products mentioned in this book.

### ACCUQUILT
Go! and Go! Baby
www.accuquilt.com

### AURIFIL
Thread
www.aurifil.com

### BIRD BRAIN DESIGNS
100 percent wool felt
www.birdbraindesigns.net

### BUTTONWOOD QUILTS
Fabric
www.buttonwoodquilts.com

### CLOVER NEEDLECRAFT
Desk needle threader
www.clover-usa.com

### DAILYCRAFTTV
Jodie's quilting how-to videos
www.DailyCraftTV.com

### DREAMWORLD NORTHWEST
Sew Steady tables
www.sewsteady.com

### THE ELECTRIC QUILT COMPANY
Premium Cotton Lawn Inkjet Fabric
www.electricquilt.com

### FONS & PORTER'S®
White mechanical pencil
www.shopfonsandporter.com

### HOBBS BONDED FIBERS
Heirloom cotton batting
www.hobbsbondedfibers.com

### PILOT PENS
Pilot FriXion
www.pilotpen.us

### QNNTV
Quilt It! The Longarm Quilting Show
www.QNNtv.com

### THE QUILT ALLIANCE
The Quilt Index
www.allianceforamericanquilts.org

### STITCHCRAFT CREATIVE QUILTING & SEWING
Fabric
www.stitchcraftboca.com

### THE WARM COMPANY
Lite Steam-A-Seam2
Steam-A-Seam2
Warm & Natural batting
www.warmcompany.com

# INDEX